Why do
Violets Shrink?

Why do Violets Shrink?

Answers to 280 Thorny Questions
on the World of Plants

CAROLINE HOLMES

SUTTON PUBLISHING

First published in the United Kingdom in 2008 by
The History Press
Cirencester Road · Chalford · Stroud · Gloucestershire · GL6 8PE

British Library Cataloguing in Publication Data
A catalogue record for this book is available from the British Library.

Hardback ISBN 978-0-7509-4628-5

Typeset in GillSans Light.
Typesetting and origination by
The History Press
Printed and bound in England.

Dedication

To Muriel and Violet Elizabeth – neither noted for
shrinking but good at putting varlets in their place

Contents

Acknowledgements

This has been one of the hardest books to write, posing the questions was the easy part, actually answering them in relevant fashion proved more challenging. Thank you first to Jaqueline Mitchell for inviting me to undertake the project and shaping up its format. Many questions just opened up further questions and I have been helped by many people to unravel seedy and dark green secrets. Special thanks to Bert Klein at the Munich Botanic Gardens and Jenny Wainwright-Klein at its mountain top Alpine Garden at Schachen. The internet is wonderful but you cannot beat scouring the shelves of libraries and engaging in obscure conversations with librarians, so huge thanks to the University and the Botanic Garden Libraries in Cambridge with special thanks to Sylvia Norton, the Natural History Museum, and the Cherokee Library and its Director Staci Catron-Sullivan in Atlanta. Thanks to Sandra Bywater who enlightened me not only on the collections in the Heritage Seed Library but on life on other planets. Miranda Chambers of DLF Trifolium Limited provided details of their researches on mycorrhizal associations.

Loving thanks to two good friends and wonderfully knowledgeable specialists – Mark Hill on mosses and Chuck Voigt on horseradish and pumpkins. Not forgetting general enlightening conversations with Erica Hunningher, Sue Minter,

Alan Gray of East Ruston Old Vicarage, Louise Allen at the Oxford Botanic Garden and Philip Norman at the Museum of Garden History. Impossible to mention individually by name but enthusiastic gratitude to botanic gardens in England, France, Germany and the States and The Eden Project where I have had my nose pressed either to their plants or their labels. Where would I be without my family, my nephew Max Bell who lent me his DVDs, my husband David triumphed again in his trawl for out of print and obscure books as well as casting his eye over these pages. Cursory dips and comments were made by my sons, Will and Nick.

Introduction

The idea of an eternal spring of trees bursting into bud, soft green blades rising, fresh scents and birdsong retains its magical associations. A flourishing pattern of sight and sound which begs a kaleidoscope of questions. Green is a colour that was believed to aid contemplation but is curiously used to describe someone in the grips of envy, and now ecowarriors fight under a green banner for a greener planet. We need to eat our greens: the plant's own green loving constituent, chlorophyll, conveniently attracts iron essential for our well being, iron reaches all parts, helping produce red blood cells, keeping our veins running smoothly, our tissues supple, hair follicles active and helps to sweep out unwanted waste.

But there is more to plants than green leaves, as the many questions and answers in this book show. Maybe not as colourful, but just as vivid and vibrant, are the extreme plants which cling to life in the harshest of conditions, many risking sporting a leaf and a flower, some not even having the sophistication to do that, in order to evade extinction. Their means of survival and attempts to flourish are as myriad as their outer appearances – plants don't do makeovers, they tenaciously evolve over millennia. Scientific research has revealed complexities that just beg more questions; under the microscope, plants are ever more extraordinary.

Across the globe, native plants have myths and legends attached to them, stories with a core of truth which provide a colourful guide on where they can be found and how man can grow, harvest and use them. Wheat and maize are legendary, clear winners in the ancient myths stakes, plants with purpose, outstripped in consumption by rice but like rice, they are global travellers. The Roman writer Ovid wrote *The Metamorphoses* which essentially are tales of godly daring, recounting how gods metamorphosed into earthly disguises to change the human world. Nymphs, shepherds, lovers and animals might find themselves protected or damned into plant form – bay, heartsease, mint or narcissus. In lands shaped by the four seasons, watching the ground spring to life, flower, seed and fall back, is in itself a metamorphosis that poses lots of questions. 'Why do violets shrink' is a literary metamorphosis, the original saying related to 'shrinking varlets' – so rather than maidenly blushes, it is a case of youthful male bashfulness. In the real world, the true violets do shrink from the clumsy attentions of busy bees in spring.

The loves and lives of plants and trees follow ingenious routes; pragmatic and practical, they make full use of intermediaries – sometimes for mutual benefit, sometimes not. Plants can help our love lives, the scent of jasmine to make you more alluring and roots and shoots to pep up your vitality. Flowering plants need to be pollinated by insects and animals such as butterflies, humming-birds, bees, mosquitoes, wasps, bats as well as ants and termites: so their flowers orchestrate sophisticated PR campaigns and offer theme park rides. In the insect world intelligence is measured by tongue length, there are record breaking tongues on insects with plants to match. Flower-pollinating bats have small ears and prodigious tongues which can be neatly curled away when not in use. Beneficial beasties in insect, avian and mammal form have helped spread plants, often lured by the scent of sexual encounters or just as incidental transport for wind blown pollen. A natural balance which has helped man subsist and inspired ethereal poetry – a curiously even weighting – but then man wants to eat more and earn more, resulting in an imbalance and some very peculiar pests.

The earliest cultivators noted and saved seed from the plants that showed the greatest yields. Renaissance gardeners and their princes prized variegated and double flowering mutants but it was not until the eighteenth century that Thomas Fairchild wrestled with his conscience and actively crossed or hybridised a Sweet William with a carnation. Nearly three hundred years later, playing God and manipulating nature's breeding programme has produced a potato with an inbuilt insecticide. Many native insects are reliant on native plants at some point in their life cycle. In flora-rich lands such as South Africa and Australia introduced plants have become thugs destroying both native flora and fauna. In Britain however, many of those introduced, especially single flowers have brought spice and variety for native insects, echoed in common names such as bee balm for Bergamot, introduced from the Americas, and Butterfly Bush for Buddleia from the Far East.

A primary human need is to eat, followed by a need for shelter, medicine and making money. Plants can fulfil all these needs and it is interesting to speculate on how many pioneering planters, observers and consumers died confirming use or uselessness – how curiously appropriate that toxic is the filling in the sandwich of intoxication. Should you find yourself on a desert island searching for food, a quick test for potential poisoning is to gently rub a leaf, fruit or fungi across the back of your wrist. A stinging sensation means go no further! A quicker but potentially more dangerous test is to pass it across your lower lip; last but not least taste it, but if you suffer a burning sensation in your mouth or throat spit it out and keep rinsing and spitting until all trace has gone.

Across the world common names provide more than a clue as to what plants look like, the purpose they serve, how they are used or abused, whether they are dangerous, and so on. One plant can be known by many vernacular names but its given name in Latin is unique and a quicker, if less exciting, guide to its parentage, appearance and habits.

On Earth seven main centres of origin for cultivated plants have been identified, Nicolay Ivanovich Vavilov revisited them in his quest to establish the roots of global genetic diversity, in his words 'to understand the "agricultural soul" of [each] country and its conditions'. He published his findings in *Five Continents;* the fifth centre he identified was Abyssinia, present day Ethiopia, long believed to be the kingdom from which the Queen of Sheba travelled to meet Solomon with wondrous plants and spices. This journey equates with space travel except that we have yet to successfully exchange green thoughts in a green shade with other planets.

Was it wishful thinking that when Uranus was discovered, its satellite moons and stars were named for characters from Shakespeare's bee-sucking, flower-strewn *A Midsummer Night's Dream*? Equally how sensible that H.G. Wells's Martians chose to land in Woking then an area noted for nurseries nurturing and propagating the treasures plant hunters were bringing back from the four corners of the earth. There are 283 questions and answers in this book that address plants and planting from the Garden of Eden to Mars for mortals and literate Martians.

1

Back to Roots

Which comes first, the **root** or the **leaf?**

When a seed germinates, it puts down a small anchor root which when established, pushes up its seedling leaf or leaves. This is the reason that gardening books tell you to create a firm seed bed, with light aerated fibrous soil on top for quick anchorage but a gentle barrier that the root pushes up that leaf through to get the food chain started, rather than wasting precious resources rooting to the centre of the earth. Seedling leaves look much the same, then strengthened by the first solid feeds of photosynthesis as the seedling leaves and spreading roots develop, the first rough leaves start to open, advertising their parentage.

Some sneaky weeds like the Bearded Darnel, *Lolium temulentum*, imitate their surroundings in order to escape detection and eradication; the seventeenth century herbalist Nicolas Culpeper described it as 'a pestilent enemy among the corn'. Until its larger seed head, or more correctly boat shaped glume with long awns (visualise a shop awning) and fruiting pales form, it looks exactly like crops such as wheat and barley, by which time weeding it out is nigh on impossible. Its seeds sit in spikelets standing edgeways on each side of the stem protected by a single elongated glume whereas wheat has its spikelets sideways against the stem with two protective outer glumes. Glumes are neither glum nor gloomy but dry, chaffy bracts typically found in the inflorescences on grasses,

2

cereals and rushes. Although modern research is exploring the possibility that darnel is nutritious, historically the darnel grains were a must to avoid when grinding corns: it caused a general trembling which led to an inability to walk and talk followed by vomiting. Recipients also suffered from impaired vision, seeing everything in a shade of green. The French common name, Ivraie, or drunkenness was apt; apparently in the South of France it was fed to restless mules to induce a comatose state. However, although the ill effects are linked to the grains, as it is a ready host for the fungus Ergot which causes the above symptoms, this is the more likely culprit. Regardless of whether the whole grain or parasitic Ergot were to blame, Bearded Darnel was classed as an agricultural menace.

Which **plants start** from **seeds?**

The simple answer is 'seed plants' but then the divisions start, depending on whether they produce naked or covered seeds. Freely accessible for pollination and sounding as though they have just done a workout, naked seeds are called gymnosperms. They produce trees like spruce, fir, larch and the cypress. Their covered counterparts have the distinctly hospital check-up name of angiosperms; in these types the seeds are enclosed in the carpel. You can find them on grasses, roses, cabbages and lilies. An apple core is a readily visible example of how a carpel develops – following pollination the carpel in apple blossoms (which are part of the rose family) becomes the core. If you collect angiosperm seeds and sow them you will notice that when the grasses and lilies germinate up comes just one simple leaf, while roses and cabbages have a pair. Here is the evidence for the next division, monocotyledon – one seedling leaf and dicotyledon – two. Most seeds have an inbuilt food sack that provides enough nutrients for the seed to establish its first shoot and root. Orchids, especially the rare Lady's Slipper Orchid, do not have this food sack, equating more to the hunter-gatherer peoples, their seeds float up into the air ready to fuse with compatible microscopic fungi which will provide the necessary nourishment. They can then fall back to earth and start germinating. No fungi, no seed set and thus an endangered species.

Why do **plants** have **flowers?**

Mostly to attract a pollinator, the flower is a specialised reproductive shoot in the form of an interactive billboard advertising its wares by attractive visuals and enticing scents. Different colours draw pollinators such as insects, birds and bats from afar and as they come into closer range their sense of smell enables precise species recognition. Some flowers offer the extra incentive of odour guides such as an odour gradient or a difference in the odour composition (pp.106-8). The flower is a whole made up of many differently named parts held around a central axis appropriately known as a receptacle. The receptacle supports four different organs: calyx, corolla, stamens and carpels whose individual parts enable the flower to fulfil the final goal of fertilisation. The advertising campaign is undertaken by the calyx and corolla, they are combined in the perianth, and, having successfully drawn in the pollinating customers, leave the stamens and carpels to fulfil the reproductive role.

The calyx is made up of the sepals which are most noticeable at bud stage, they act like a green cape enclosing and protecting the juvenile flower, then as the flower opens they fall back to form the understorey for the petals. The corolla assembles single or multiple numbers of petals which are usually the conspicuous, brightly coloured element of the advertising campaign. The perianth, i.e. the calyx and corolla, are also known as accessory flower parts because they are not directly concerned in the act of reproduction. Whereas the last two organs which lie at the core of the flower, the stamens and carpels, are known as the essential flower parts because they are the active beneficiaries of the marketing campaign. The Venerable Bede writing in the early seventh century poetically described the stamens of Madonna lilies, *Lilium candidum*, as sparkling like divine lights. When they leave yellow stains on noses and clothes the descriptions become less poetic.

What are the **technical** parts of **stamens** and **carpels?**

Stamens are technically known as microsporophylls, collectively the androecium. Each one is made up of a filament or stalk bearing an anther; this is where the microspores, the staining, sparkling lights better known as pollen grains, are produced. Finally, in the centre of the flower is the gynoecium, comprising one or more megasporophylls; tripping off the tongue more easily is their alternative name of carpels. A carpel carries style and stigma in its reproductive parts, as it consists of an ovary, a terminal prolongation called the style, and bears the stigma which is the receptive surface for pollen grains. The ovary contains a varying number of ovules which after fertilization develop into seed.

How
do **flowers** get
their **colour?**

Flowers evolved from the green leaves that protected the ovules and pollen bearing organs about 250 million years ago. Gradually the green pigments faded leaving the yellow or, if further faded, white, which started to take on the shape of a flower. At the same time beetles were evolving, supping on nutritious pollen and drinking the drops of sticky liquid that were intended to catch wind-borne pollen, in time they were joined by two winged flies. In the Cretaceous period about 130 million years ago bees, butterflies and birds burst onto the scene looking for bright beacons, so flowers revolutionised their colours and structures to accommodate these new pollinators. The visual spectrum of an insect extends from yellow through to ultra violet whereas birds and mammals see from red through to violet. Insects favour the colourful intensity of yellows, blues and ultra violets and those making day time visits look for the brightest colours. The reward is that the complex sugars, fats and amino acids contained in nectar stimulate egg production in their pollinators. As nectar was the drink of the gods, early botanists decided to give the sweet liqueur that bees turn into honey the same name.

What do **red flowers** attract?

Birds are attracted to red flowers because their sight is sensitive to red. Red flowers are most commonly found in North and South America as well as in the tropical areas of the Old World but rarely in Europe. Red flowers hold no interest for insects. And the poppy? We see red but bees see ultra-violet.

What is the **floral** formula?

A quick code to identify flower parts. A buttercup is $K_5C_5A\infty G\underline{\infty}$. It is a flower with a calyx – K – with 5 free sepals, a corolla – C – with 5 free petals, an infinite number of stamens in the androecium – A, and finally an infinite number of carpels in the gynoecium – G, and underlined to show it has a superior ovary, superior in the sense that it is clearly visible.

What would **I find** if **invited** into a **plant's cell?**

First admire the walls made of cellulose whose fibrous nature, especially in cotton, linen and even New Zealand flax, are the very fabric of the textile industry. Some primary walls undergo further improvement, not least in the use of technical language, such as lignification of the fibres for increased strength and rigidity; or cuticularisation (think of the cuticles on your nails) of epidermal (outermost) walls or suberisation (a combination of oxidisation and condensation) of cork cells rendering them impermeable to water. Should you be lucky enough to voyage into a fungi cell, the walls are made of chitin which is a nitrogen-containing polysaccharide with long fibrous molecules that provide structure and energy reserves.

Having penetrated the primary and, if necessary, secondary walls, hard at work will be the protoplast actively metabolising the substances. The cytoplasm or inner structure contains furniture shaped accessories: looking like a sofa, the mitochondria, like coffee tables, the lysosomes and like stools, centrosomes. Finally through membrane veils, the nucleus lurks at the centre surrounded by a private wall; enter this and you will meet two darker nucleoli awaiting the chance to go to their own dance of the seven veils, that of the chromosomes – full instructions in Mating and Dating (p.122). From these small cells the greater structures of the branches, leaves, flowers and other parts of plants are formed.

Why are **plants** green?

Because of a pigment called chlorophyll, which is found in several forms in algae and higher plants in the part of their cells called chloroplasts. Not just a pretty colour, chlorophyll can capture light, harness its energy in its chloroplast and initiate the process that turns it into chemical power – better known as photosynthesis. Lack of light can cause chlorosis, a disease characterised by the yellowing of otherwise healthy green parts; lime-induced chlorosis is the term used if the soil has too much lime which prevents the plants from taking up nutrients and causes them to look like they need a bit of sunshine. This has nothing to do with golden or variegated leaves although these may be less efficient at photosynthesising.

Is there more to photosynthesis than light and green?

Yes, the chloroplast acts as the plant's engine, absorbing light energy and converting it into chemical energy in one part, while another uses the chemical energy to reduce the carbon dioxide to form carbohydrates. Scientists from the University of Leicester have taken to the skies to watch nature in action from space; streaks of carbon dioxide are visibly hoovered up during the growing season by vegetation in Siberia, North America, Northern Europe and India. Out of sight the green light action requires nifty footwork in the form of healthy hairy roots. Manufacturing calls for fluid intake and, in an action called osmosis, the stronger brew within the plant draws liquid from the soil through a semi-permeable membrane in the root hairs. Soil needs fibre in its diet to retain water, anchor root systems and encourage root hairs – the hairier the better. In the process the rising water oxidises and is released as oxygen, which is why the great tracts of forest, greenery and algae are called the lungs of our planet.

What is **cellulose?**

It is the principle structural molecule in all plants making up the fibrous part of the cell walls. When the plant is young it is flexible to allow room for the cells to grow. For example, wood is about 50 per cent cellulose whilst cotton is pure cellulose – cellulose is about all that remains in dead plant cells after dehydration.

Can you **wipe your feet** on a **microbial** mat?

No, a microbial mat is a primitive form of bacteria, known as cyanobacteria or blue-green algae (sometimes orange or black) that forms a community of many species known as a microbial mat. Looking unexcitingly like scum, these algae are actually some of the oldest life-forms on Earth and may have been one of the original sources of oxygen. The special attribute of cyanobacteria is its ability to use sunlight to convert carbon dioxide into energy-rich sugar, generating oxygen as a waste product. Such photosynthesizers anchor the food chain, providing sustenance for all higher organisms.

Microbial mats are at their best in the harsh terrain of Dry Valley on Antarctica and flourish in the hypersaline waters of Shark Bay, Australia. Survivors of the first living communities, stromatolite reefs still flourish in Shark Bay as they did throughout the globe 3.5 billion years ago. Taking up the top few inches, a velvety microbial mat grows in fine layers that include a crown of oxygen-producing photosynthetic cyanobacteria, a middle section of bacteria that can tolerate some oxygen and sunlight, and, at the bottom, bacteria that thrive only in the absence of oxygen and sunlight. Sediments trapped in the mat bind with calcium carbonate from the water, constantly building up the solid rock base. To gain access to sunlight – and to keep from getting cemented in – the organisms move upwards through the sediments. Evolving in an oxygen-free atmosphere, the first photosynthetic bacteria consumed and gave off other gases. Then, like a Greek tragedy, mutant offspring began to produce oxygen, poisoning the parents and stunting the growth of competing microbes. As the air became rich in oxygen, the offspring took over the surface while the parents retreated. The red and blue pigments in algae which assist photosynthesis are called phycobilins, and transfer the light energy they absorb to the chlorophyll so that it can be put to use. The study of algae is called phycology.

Who **roams** the pastures of **the sea?**

Plants of the ocean are nearly as productive acre for acre as those on dry land and are the first living link in the food chain. First let's meet the plankton who passively flow back and forth seeking illumination to a depth of 300ft in order to function: in their plant chlorophyll-bearing form they are called phytoplankton, providing nourishment for their animal relations zooplankton. In turn zooplankton are then prey to a panoply of bigger creatures, notably whales. Chlorophyll-bearing plants, such as diatoms are also known as nannoplankton, flagellates and blue green algae – of whom more later.

How do deep **water algae** photosynthesise?

They use the tiny amount of sunlight available by growing rod like structures called chlorosomes which contain thousands of light-harvesting pigment molecules. A wonder of adaptation, scientists are trying to replicate chlorosomes to tap solar-energy more efficiently – current systems are about 10 per cent efficient, the deep water algae are 97 per cent successful. Although marine plants' biomass is less than one percent that of land plants, they contribute almost the same amount to the

Earth's total photosynthesis, i.e. absorbing carbon dioxide and exuding oxygen.

Why do **plant stems** bend towards the **window?**

Plants are seeking the best light source in an action called tropism. It is most noticeable in indoor plants. Whether as an aid to or in conjunction with this summons to the light, the cells in the stem tips on the shady side elongate.

Are there plants that **cannot** photosynthesise?

Saprophytes are a group of plants that have no chlorophyll and cannot use the sun's rays as their usual source of food. The world's largest flower, *Rafflesia arnoldii*, comes into this category.

Instead these plants devise other ways to obtain their food from the organic elements in humus with the help of fungi, such as the Birds Nest Orchid or the parasitic Broomrapes, more of whom in Peculiar Pests (see p. 184). Another saprophyte that does not photosynthesise is the Snowplant (*Scarcodes sanguinea*); it is also described as an epiparasite because it receives its nourishment from parasitizing the roots of neighbouring plants and other decaying organic matter. It is only found in the Yellow Pine and Red Fir forest of California and Southern Oregon and is protected by Californian law. As the name suggests, it emerges brightly through the snow and stands like a red Christmas decoration after the snows have melted. Its red strappy fronds, sometimes described as asparagus-like, then flower and form seeds.

The so-called 'living stones' *Lithops* – from the Greek *lithos* stone and *opsis* appearance – are succulent stemless perennials. They blend in with rocks and pebbles in sand, gravel and occasionally clay soils, and from their pebble-centres a tiny pair of insignificant leaves and a solitary yellow or white flower emerges. Minimal photosynthesis takes place through these 'windows' where the light can penetrate the chloroplasts.

What is the **difference** between tree transpiration and **respiration?**

Transpiring is much the same as sweating. Trees transpire through their leaves, which is one of the reasons why trees and plants have evolved leaf shapes adapted to their native climate. Tropical leaves in humid climates tend to be bigger with greater transpiration, deciduous trees help themselves by losing their leaves in winter, and the needle leaves of conifers are ideal for extreme cold. Conifers have also developed thick, tough skins to slow down their transpiration. Leaves may limit water loss from their tissues by means of reduced surface area or by developing a protective coating like the leathery and wax coated Bergenia, ivies and buckthorns. The leaves of heathers, rosemary and ornamental grasses are needle-like or lanceolate (spear-like) to conserve water. Tiny thymes and the delicate screen of leaves on the Tamarix both have imbricated or overlapping leaves that look like scales. The finely cut and indented leaves of herbs like wormwood, fennel and cotton lavender are tolerant of dry Mediterranean type summers. Similarly the hairy or woolly leafed plants like the horned poppy, Jerusalem sage and Senecio withstand drying winds.

The ability of *Glaucium flavum*, the horned poppy, to withstand salt laden sea winds is poignantly expressed by Robert Bridges in the poem dedicated to her.

> A poppy grows upon the shore,
> Bursts her twin cup in summer late;
> Her leaves are glaucous – green and hoar,
> Her petals yellow – delicate.
> She has no lovers like the red,
> That dances with the noble corn;

Her blossoms on the waves are shed,
Where she stands shivering and forlorn.

Succulents include plants whose fleshy interiors enable them to withstand some of the most arid areas in the world.

Respiration occurs night and day from all its living parts as the tree breathes in carbon dioxide and breathes out oxygen. After harvest even in lower cooler storage conditions, apples and pears continue to lose moisture, commercial stores slow down the process of respiration by raising the carbon dioxide level in temperatures between 5°C (40°F) and 10°C (40°F). You can do a mini version of this by wrapping apples and pears in plastic bags and storing them in the vegetable rack of the refrigerator. I, myself, idly hang apples from our six trees in plastic bags in my open porch in East Anglia and reckon that only about 20 per cent rot over 5-6 months. The fruit picked first lasts longest so start using the last pickings.

What do **roots** give to the **soil**, or do they **just take?**

Soil erosion by wind is at its worst on flat land especially when devoid of vegetation; planting hedges helps reduce wind speed and always ensuring the soil has plant cover, will prevent erosion. On slopes where water does not percolate into the soil it simply washes it away. The dense binding root mass of grasses such as maram, is more effective than trees in slowing erosion, especially of shorelines. The loss of trees through human deforestation in the Himalayas, has adversely affected the flow of rivers such as the Ganges which indirectly may affect the lives and livelihoods of over 400 million people

Plants in the pea and bean family fix nitrogen from the atmosphere and store it in their root nodules, hence their importance in the four-crop rotation used in vegetable gardens and agriculture. Digging in green manures and composted garden waste aids penetration and acts as a soil conditioner that improves the structure for better drainage and aeration.

Roots, like leaves, adapt to what the soil has to offer; some such as Sea Holly, *Eryngium*, and Californian Tree Poppy, *Romneya*, can forage into the subsoil for water. Root penetration is helped by a process called flocculation whereby the electrical charges on colloids are neutralized, allowing the particles to join together into much larger aggregates. Clay and sand are at the two ends of the colloidal spectrum, colloids are particles that are 'suspended' in the soil's solutions: clay is formed from ultra-fine colloids which is why in its raw state it is so good for pottery – it sticks together making it hard for roots to penetrate. On the other hand sand colloids are so large that water and nutrients drain away too quickly. The effect on roots of heavy clay is that they are stubby, while sand makes them very long and straggly.

Light showers of rain and dew call for rapid reaction from a web of surface roots in shrubs such as lavenders, *Lavandula*, and tamarisk or salt cedar, *Tamarix*. Be prepared is the motto of the Bearded Iris whose rhizomes act as water storage organs. Many of the bulbs that brighten spring gardens when rain is plentiful die back into dormancy, hiding underground until autumn and winter rains awaken and prepare them for their flowery show.

Can **roots survive** in the **air** or under **water?**

Yes to both. A group of plants called epiphytes such as various lichens, mosses and orchids, typically found in regions of high humidity, use other plants as supports and have aerial roots which absorb the moisture from the atmosphere. Plants do not die as a result of water but the lack of oxygen in waterlogged conditions. Mangroves are specialized plants with some eleven members in the genera, of which the best known is the genus *Rhizophora*, that grow in swamps inundated by brackish or sea water in tropical and sub tropical regions. Special adaptations include the self-explanatory stilt roots above the water which support the trees, acting as respiratory organs, and the pneumatophores which are air-filled apogeotropic roots that look like knobbly knees. Normal roots are positively geotropic, in other words they grow vertically downwards, whereas apogeotropic ones do their own thing, i.e. growing vertically upwards. Various ferns, palms and screwpines can also form part of mangrove swamps.

The Swamp or Bald Cypress is hardier, surviving cold winters in Northern Europe and far inland along the Mississippi bottomlands in Indiana. It has supporting flange-like outgrowths known as buttressed roots and pneumatophores which give the impression that it is marching along the banks of the rivers or lakes where it is planted. The one most frequently seen in European parks *Taxodium distichum* has the added benefit that it is both tolerant of city air and the high pH of chalk streams.

What is soil **pH?**

It is the measurement of the acidity or alkalinity of soil on a scale from pH1 to pH14. In general plants grow best on soils between pH 5.5 and 7.5, pH 7 is classed as neutral and 6.5 optimum for plant growth. Normal soils are unable to fall below pH 4 but the chemical breakdown of colliery soil generates acids that take the soil down to an unsustainable pH of 1 or 2. High pH's mean that plants struggle to find minerals such as manganese, boron, phosphorus and in some soils, calcium. At a low pH plants may suffer a shortage of phosphorous and a toxicity of manganese and aluminium. One of the most spectacular displays of carnivorous plants can be seen at the Atlanta Botanical Garden on a soil of pH 4.5, the trapped insects compensating for the negligible nutrition from the soil.

Do soils **yawn** when they **get tired?**

Heavy clay soils open up into yawning gaps in times of drought but tired soils are usually hungry, lacking in fibre and depleted of nutrients. This can be caused by overcropping where soil has been worked but not manured with dung or compost or fertilised by a green manure such as clover or alfalfa which is then dug in. Tired soil cannot retain water effectively so is subject to erosion by flash flooding.

How fast
does **grass** grow?

It grows fastest in temperate areas as the temperature rises in combination with adequate water. Water meadows used to be lightly flooded in spring so that the sun would warm the shallow water which in turn fed the grasses, providing early pasture for grazing animals. Lawns reach maximum growth in late spring and early summer before the seasonal heat and drought slow them down. The new green spikes of bulbs are triggered by day length but with climate change bluebells are finding themselves flooded by high speed grass. If you want the wilder meadow look the prettier Greater Knapweed will compete effectively with grass and can flower for up to three months. The Yellow Rattle grows semi-parasitically on grasses, thus hindering its growth while providing bright splashes of yellow.

What is **peat?**

The peat mosses, Bog moss, *Sphagnum acutifolium*, and Hypnum moss grow in shallow lakes or wet hollows in marshes where the soil is sour and low in nutrients. As the newer growths form, they press down the older moss which results in the formation of peat. Soft and thick Sphagnum moss is easily distinguished by its pale green colour, it can also be pink and even red. The fibrous quality of peat stems from the spiral fibres loosely coiled in the leaf-cells; rushes, sedges and horsetails also add to the dark-brown mix. Large scale peatlands form as a result of rapid plant growth and high moisture content creating anaerobic conditions which can create deposits tens of metres thick over large areas. Highland peats are usually formed from mosses and the more compact, homogeneous lowland peats originate from sedges and rushes. When drained they can form very productive lands such as the Cambridgeshire fenlands.

What makes a bryology tapestry?

Mosses: the study of mosses is called bryology. Very few mosses have common names so although tiny in structure they are saddled with lengthy Latin nomenclature. Look carefully for the far from ugly weft and warp: there is the soft nap velvet-like *Plagiothecium*; the silky brocade of *Brotherella* and shiny ribbons of *Mnium*.

The tapestry-like smooth surface is a clever device: the closer to the ground a plant (or indeed a human sheltering from the wind) grows the less it is affected by air turbulence. The less it is exposed to breezes the more water it retains – essential for rootless mosses. Sometimes, the tapestry is broken by thread-like stems with a terminal capsule containing spores, called sporophytes, which spring up when the moss needs to shake its spores into the wind. The sporophytes grow up away from the 'boundary layer' near the ground into the 'turbulent zone' which shakes their heads and scatters their spores. The spores germinate into male and female shoots which develop antheridia containing sperm and archegonia with the eggs at the end of their respective stems. Moss sperms or male gametes are coiled like corkscrews with two tails correctly described as motile by-flagella. These sperm swim in a springing style, a sort of hybrid butterfly/crawl stroke, across a water droplet to fuse with the egg on the female plant and so achieve fertilisation.

One of the commonest mosses *Mnium hornum* grows around tree bases, rotting wood, peat and rock ledges has male and female parts on separate plants. The males are clustered into a rosette-like structure and the females form hanging fruiting capsules on long red stalks in spring.

On walls, pavements and compacted soil in Britain you may find the Moonworts *Botrychium lunaria. B. capillare, Bryum argenteum*, all of which have shaggy catkin-like stems and fruits from autumn through to spring.   Sounding as though it should be growing on brickwork, Grout, *Pohlia carnea*, is happiest in the damp clay soils of stream and river banks. It keeps out of drying breezes by only growing 1cm tall with delicate oval leaves that are shorter and more rounded near the stem bases. The sporophytes have a ring of orange-red teeth looking like tiny feeding teats and the fruit capsules are either horizontal or hanging. Grout's close relative *P. nutans*, a traditional coloniser of heathland, moors, peat banks, woodland and rotting stumps, has adapted to growing on old industrial sites especially lead mine waste. It sends up bright orange or red stalks which hold up capsules that start green gradually becoming pale orange brown.

What is the **difference** between **mosses** and **clubmosses?**

Mosses, mostly known as bryophytes, have no secondary cells and are fairly uniform in their structure. Instead of roots, mosses have rhizoids that only anchor the undercarriage or substratum that supports the closely arranged leaves and stem that we see. In addition, there is a distinct central conducting strand of elongated cells running through the stem. Club mosses are proper modern vascular plants, further down the evolutionary trail, which have roots with which they transport water. They are grouped with ferns and horsetails as pteridophytes. Clubmosses are in the *Lycopodium* family but also have common names: such as the Fir Clubmoss – *L. selago*, the Stag's Horn Clubmoss – *L.clavatum*, the Alpine clubmoss – *L.alpinum* and the Lesser clubmoss, *Selaginella selaginoides.*

How
does **tree bark** form?

It is formed from the protective, corky tissues of dead cells which are present on the outside of older stems and roots of woody plants and trees. Bark may consist of cork only, or, when other layers of cork are formed at successively deeper levels, it may consist of alternating layers of cork and dead cortex or phloem tissue. With a structure like a series of sieve tubes, phloem is in two parts: older and active, the

latter busily conducts sugars, proteins and mineral ions. Apart from the winter bark colour of the young stems of dogwoods and willows, the most famous bark product must be that of the evergreen cork oak, *Quercus suber*. Its bark is 15cm thick and deeply fissured and has been 'mined' for cork for centuries.

How do **fruits** ripen?

First it is worth noting that plants sense a colour beyond our vision termed 'far-red' which they take as a signal to increase shoot growth. Tests have been done mulching tomatoes with a plastic that reflects far-red, with the result that, sensing serious competition, tomatoes grow bigger and ripen earlier. Plants prefer lots of sunshine at every stage, sunshine helps to ripen the wood which in turn promotes fruit bud development that, frosts, drought and tempests permitting, will swell into fruits. Sunshine in conjunction with gentle rain and/or a moisture-retentive soil adds colour, taste and sweetness as well. Discrimination is essential if you want a dish of dessert fruit. The luscious sweetness of figs, apricots, peaches, nectarines and grapes will be ensured by allocating them the choicest, sunniest spot. Crops of culinary fruits for winter dishes of warming apple crumbles and pear pies can be achieved in shadier spots.

What is a
sunny spot?

One that basks in sunshine for at least half of the day. West-facing sites tend to be warmer and the fruit takes on a mellow yellow as the sun sets. Potash is sometimes called artificial sunshine so overcast years can be brightened for fruits by applying potash in the form of bonemeal in the previous autumn.

Bending exercises carried out whilst the wood is still supple are also beneficial, helping achieve an expanding waistband of mature fruit. Branches and shoots of trees such as apples and pears are tied down into near horizontal positions which reduce the vigour of young shoots and ensure better cropping of older wood. Sounding more like some sort of interior decoration, bending plum trees in this manner is called festooning while grapes use the Geneva Double Curtain. The GDC as it is known in viticultural circles is dependent on very strong curtain poles the size of telegraph poles or railway sleepers. It is suited to mechanised grape growing as there is no need for summer pruning or bending and the machines can operate between the vines, making gangs of pickers and pruners unnecessary. The disadvantage is that the fruits miss out on the radiant heat from the soil and yields per hectare are about one third of traditionally planted vineyards. It is popular in America for vigorous vines. In medieval times grape vines were trained over arbours and seats and described as forming a living curtain.

How can you **tell**
the difference
between a
fruit bud
and a **leaf bud?**

Fruit buds are plumper while leaf buds are small and narrower. The vegetative bud normally only produces new shoots but under unusual circumstances can produce rather weak flowers. The terminal bud is exactly that, the last bud produced during the growing season on the end of a shoot.

Do **seeds sleep?**

Yes, many seeds have a dormant or sleeping period, when they are viable but in a resting condition which sometimes lasts for years. It has evolved as a safeguard to protect seeds from germinating in unfavourable conditions, such as the autumn which would leave tender vulnerable offspring to be wiped out in winter. Safely dormant in a process called stratification the cold temperatures of winter trigger an expectation of spring warmth and germination. This is why it is recommended to put seeds in damp sand in a polythene bag or plastic box in a refrigerator for six to eight weeks to fool the seeds into thinking they have been through a winter. Some will germinate at these low temperatures, others wait until the container is placed somewhere warmer.

Birds have a reputation for increasing the germination of seeds, in fact their digestive systems clean the seeds of the outer fruit, for example, in hedgerow plants such as elder, hawthorn and yew. They then drop, in all senses, the seeds away from the parent plant thus increasing the seedling's chances of reaching full maturity.

Do seeds **imbibe?**

Indeed and retain the word imbibition to describe it, an action perfectly encapsulated in the old phrase 'To lie in imbibition' for people or things left to 'lie a soak or a steep'. It is essential for a seed to soak, imbue and imbibe moisture in preparation for germination. Some hard seeded native plants in the Legume family take weeks to imbibe but they can be helped in two ways. Firstly, by stratification as described above or by scarification which is not nearly as frightening as it sounds: the seeds are simply rubbed with sandpaper until the seed coat is grazed without damaging the embryo seed inside.

Do **flower** scents have **rhythms?**

Yes, and close observation has helped the perfume industry to extract scents at optimum times. Flowers emit scent from all or any one of their parts – petals, sepals, pollen or nectar. In the day time the scent attracts flies, beetles, bees and butterflies while night-time flowers tend to be more heavily and sweetly scented to attract nocturnal pollinators such as moths and bats. The bee orchid wafts the unmistakeable scent of a female bee

to lure unwitting drones. A typical floral fragrance may contain between five and one hundred and fifty different types of volatile odour molecules whose composition and intensity can vary rhythmically. The Damask rose 'Quatre Saisons' is grown primarily for oil production and its scent is emitted in peaks and troughs associated with periods of light and dark. The glorious scent of lilies of the valley so easily appreciated on the air cannot be extracted by conventional methods; its French name *muguet* is used to describe the lily of the valley scent actually extracted from the winter flower Mahonia.

If I **transplanted** a plant from the southern **hemisphere** to the **northern,** would it change its **seasonality** overnight?

First, in simple terms, any transplant has to adjust to its new surroundings, put out new roots to establish a source of water and nutrients and new leaves to complete the process of photosynthesis. Tropical plants can be moved within the tropical regions north and south of the equator without difficulty – the conditions being the same. Growers outside the tropics replicate the conditions in palm and glass houses. The oldest pot plant at Kew is a cycad, *Encephalartos altensteinii*, which Francis Masson brought back from South Africa in 1775 – still to be seen in the Palm House.

South Africa has supplied northern hemisphere gardens with wonderfully colourful flowers such as the Gazania. At home this 'Treasure Flower' flowers in September and has decided to retain its habits, so Gazanias, usually treated as annuals, but with climate change likely to be able to stay in their beds, are invaluable sources of bright colours from the end of July onwards. Gertrude Jekyll used them 'to nearly repeat' the colour of her orange lilies. The South African aloes at the Oxford Botanic Garden continue to flower in accordance with their origins, so this necessitates careful protection of the blossoms in winter. The so-called 'winter flowering heathers' that adorn British gardens were almost entirely introduced from South Africa. In principle deciduous trees and shrubs will lose their leaves in autumn dictated by growth through the summer and then a drop in temperature, but may also retain their original flowering time.

2

Myths and
Legends

Who is **immortalised** in our morning **cereals?**

The Roman goddess Ceres, goddess of corn crops – wheat, barley, oats – the staff of life and centrepiece of western civilisation. She was the sister of Jupiter, mother of Persephone and a legendary dynamo. The torches with which she searched for the lost grain, carried off by the winter frost, and raised it to flower again, are still burning on our altars. Ovid's description in his *Metamorphoses*, translated by Arthur Golding in 1565, harvests her vitality in words:

'Dame Ceres first to break the earth with plough the manner found; she first made corn and stover soft to grow

upon the ground; she first made laws. For all these things we are to Ceres bound.'

She can still be glimpsed in many grand gardens in statue form complete with her attribute of ears of corn, usually wheat and barley, wound in a wreath around her head or in her hand sometimes accompanied by poppies.

What flower
is also sacred to **Ceres?**

The poppy, corn-rose is one of its traditional English names. In fact, she is goddess of all food grain bearing grasses originating in Central Asia into the Far East – barley, buckwheat, millet, oats, rice, rye and wheat. The Gallo-Romans brewed a golden beer from barley which they named in honour of Ceres *cerevisia*, the root of today's Spanish name for beer *cervesa*. Demeter is her Greek equivalent. In German mythology she is known as Bertha organising the winds and clouds, helping reapers and acting like a werewolf to protect the growing cornfields.

What links **barley, beards** and **beer?**

Barley's latin name is *Hordeum vulgare*, which derives from *horridus* that translates as bearded with bristles, and indeed the awned glumes are long and bristle like. The Chinese read this as a symbol of potency, the Greeks trained their athletes on barley mush and the bread in the 'Feeding of the Five Thousand' was barley loaves.

So **who** first **fermented** the grain?

The Egyptians ascribed it to their god of agriculture, Osiris who made a decoction of barley that had germinated with the sacred waters of the Nile. However, he was called away on more urgent business and the germinating barley was left out in the sun. On his return it had fermented. Never one given to waste, he decided to drink it and was pleasantly surprised. Generous in spirit, he shared the new-found secret and beer was born. The first true recipes for brewing beer from barley and/or emmer wheat have been found as a cruciform inscription on a Babylonian library brick dating back to 2,800 BC. The seventeenth century astrologer-physician Nicholas Culpeper wrote that barley was a notable plant under the sign of Saturn and was 'unwholesome' for people of a melancholy disposition.

Hearing the first cuckoo in spring is a competitive activity in the British Isles still attracting annual column inches; according to tradition it was the moment to sow barley, in rather warmer Egypt the time to harvest it. When the cuckoo sees barley ears in Britain she departs.

Why does Apollo wear a garland of bay leaves around his head?

Back in the mists of time the young nymph Daphne was taking a sylvan walk when Apollo tried to force his attentions on her. She called the gods to protect her chastity and her body was saved from violation by being metamorphosed into a bay tree, *Lauris nobilis*. Ashamed by his ungallant behaviour Apollo cast aside his godly crown of oak leaves, symbol of his powerful father Jupiter, and formed a new coronet from bay leaves. When the Roman and Sabine peoples managed to agree a peaceable union they planted two bay trees in front of the Roman Temple of Mars. Roman and later emperors, including Napoleon, were routinely depicted in statuary and on coins resplendent in bay coronets, Tiberius Caesar believed it protected him from lightening.

What words have grown from these laurus roots?

The international examination called the *baccalaureat* and from this bachelor as well as the poet laureate. Alexander Pope in his sarcastic *Catalogue of Greens* writes of 'Modern poets in Bays, somewhat blighted, to be disposed of a pennyworth'.

Conveniently the bay can successfully be clipped into formal shapes and woven into garlands. The laurels you may choose to rest on stem from the bay, however, the English laurel shrub is actually *Prunus laurocerasus* introduced by the Tudors for a hardier evergreen look in their gardens.

How did the **acanthus leaf** get to the **top** of the **Corinthian** column?

According to the Roman architect and military engineer, Vitruvius, one day a young man called Callimachus was walking through a Greek graveyard when he spotted the grave of a young girl with a plant basket covered with a tile on top of it. The tile had been placed there to protect the plant during the winter but in the spring warmth the leaves had started into growth, curling under the tile and over the basket. Callimachus was moved by the beauty of the leaves and the sentiment of new life springing on the grave of maidenly innocence. The plant was an acanthus and so provided the motif for the ornate Corinthian column tops which remain symbolic of rebirth and female virtue. As the Corinthian column represents the highest form of beauty and purity it is used to indicate the aesthetic high point of a building or room.

Today their leaves are also touched with gold. The variety Hollard's Gold pokes its buttercup yellow shoots out of the ground as a preliminary to the glowing golden leaves that follow lighting up dark corners in the garden. Less classical and more beastly *Acanthus* also has the common name of Bear's Breeches because the flowers look like the fur on a bear's back legs.

Why is the **olive** a symbol of **peace?**

In the Old Testament the dove returning to Noah after the turmoil of the Great Flood carried an olive sprig in its beak, later Moses exempted men cultivating olives from military service. Olives have been growing in the Mediterranean area since 3,000 BC and today there are trees reputed to be 1,000 years old.

These symbols of peace gained potency because of their longevity combined with the fact that traditionally it took twenty years before they cropped commercially. Unless you lived in a time of peace there was no point in planting an olive grove whose fruits you might never savour. They are represented by the goddess of war, wisdom, arts and science, Minerva, who was not born of woman but sprang pure and undefiled from Jupiter's head. A poetic juxtaposition of war and peace, the just war once settled opens an era of prosperous peace and a chance to plant and harvest your olive grove. The olive oil coating your salad is symbolic of goodness and purity.

Who **first** took **tea?**

There are several ancient tales of tea: one relates to Bodhidharma, Patron of the Tea Plant. Bodhidharma was an Indian prince who accompanied by the third son of King Kosjusva and a Buddhist monk and missionary, set sail for China to teach the doctrines of Gautama. The monk, Ta-Mo vowed he would not sleep until Bodhidharma had fulfilled his mission, so he taught, prayed and meditated maintaining his wakefulness for many years until the fateful day when he fell into sleep. On awakening he cut off his eyelids in mortification at his weakness and threw them to the ground. Buddha knowing him to be a good and honourable man changed them into a plant that would ensure wakefulness, the tea plant – *Camellia sinensis*.

Appropriately it is the top young leaves that make the finest brew and curiously the flowers have the colour and scent of a fragrant freshly infused pot of tea

Tea today can be taken green or black to aid wakefulness with the knowledge that it contains antioxidants that help protect against heart disease, strokes and cancer. It is a bitter, astringent herb that stimulates the nervous system with diuretic and bactericidal effects. However, you can have too much of a good thing and in excess tea consumption can become addictive, cause constipation, palpitations, irritability and insomnia.

Which plant
is the **earthly** rainbow?

The Iris, named after the messenger of the gods who used the rainbow as an intergalactic slide when bearing missives from the heavens to classical heroes on earth. The landing marks on the falls, three dropped petals, carry the same hues as the rainbow while the standards maintain the iris's chosen colour. Just to confuse matters the iris was called a gladioli in classical times as its leaves look like a sword.

What **colours**
does **corn** come in?

Many colours. According to legend they were first offered by Yaapa, the Mockingbird who placed different kinds of corn in front of the Indian tribes. The Hopi people chose blue which was the last and smallest ear of corn. This meant the Hopi would have a long-lasting but hard life, they still grow blue corn and it is their symbol. The Hopi use corn in several of their ceremonies as the emblematic representation of life. All Hopi children receive their name from their paternal aunts in a ceremony where a perfect ear of white corn, *tsotsmingwu*, is passed four times over a twenty day old baby while it is fed their holy blue corn mash.

The Navajo took yellow ears, the Sioux picked the white, the Havasupai selected red, the Ute wanted the flint whilst the Apache chose the corn with the longest ears. In fact Native Americans bred the types still in use today – pop, dent, flint, flour, and sweet.

How did the feminine touch save the Huron Indians from starvation?

Famine was rife and the Great Spirit realised the Huron Indians needed help so he sent a woman. She set to work quickly, touching the ground first with her right hand, the soil yielded potatoes. She touched the ground with her left hand and up sprung maize corn. The Huron Indians gratefully harvested the crops while the woman sat back on the ground and watched contentedly. Her mission successfully accomplished, she simply disappeared but they discovered that where she had sat there was tobacco growing.

After the Indian princess Pocohontas saved the life of and later married the Englishman John Rolfe, he crossed her Indian strain of tobacco with a variety that was grown in the West Indies. In 1613 he introduced his new mild Virginia tobacco to England, by 1620 over 40,000 tons of this Virginia Gold had been shipped into England. Rolfe's account of how he was shipwrecked on one of his transatlantic crossings inspired Shakespeare to write *The Tempest*.

The original 'Huron' trio of potatoes, maize and tobacco were described for the first time in English literature by John Gerard in 1597: 'Of Potato's of Virginia. . . .The Indians call this plant Pappus' wrongly believing that the potato originated in North not South America; he unenthusiastically writes that 'Turkie Corne . . . doth nourish far lesse than either wheat, rie, barly, or otes'. He advises to sow it in March and April to ripen in September if 'the summer falleth out to be faire and hot'. The multi-coloured grained varieties of sweetcorn actually seem only fully to develop when there is a consistently hot summer

Apart from being amusingly immortalised in a ditty by Bob Newhart for introducing tobacco, Walter Raleigh planted potatoes on his Irish estates where they became the staple crop of the poor until the Irish Potato Famine. As Governments issue health warnings in the fight to stop tobacco smoking, lower salt and fat levels in packets of potato crisps and popcorn, jacket potatoes and corn on the cob get the health green light. Aside from being good to eat, maize starch is being used to make biodegradable plastics for packaging, cutlery, carrier bags, nappies and tyres.

What **connects**
crows and **corn?**

In one of the legends of the Narranganset Indians, the arrival of a crow from the south west of their hunting grounds is recounted. In one ear he had tucked a kernel of corn and in the other a bean. The Narranganset planted both seeds and they flourished, so in recognition of the bird's benevolence, crows were always allowed safe passage across their lands and were never molested.

What are
the **Three Sisters?**

The Lenape Indians lived around present-day Pennsylvania and while the men of the tribe hunted, their women farmed a crop combination that ensured their survival. Three staple vegetables known as The Three Sisters were grown which can still be cultivated to make an ornamental edible feature in smaller domestic gardens. The Three Sisters stand tall, bedecked in vegetable buttons and bows, frills and flounces. Corn kernels are sown at the centre to create a sturdy core support, around them scarlet runner beans seeds are set which will scramble up and be supported by the corn stalks, finally pumpkins whose abundant green leaves and orangey-yellow flowers form a flouncy petticoat. The high water table and hot summers helped to ensure good crop yields which could be eaten fresh or dried for winter use.

Attractive and nutritious: the corn is gluten-free, a source of fibre and vitamin B; the beans are high in vitamin C and help the body in absorbing iron; the pumpkin is high in Vitamins B1 and E, has excellent antioxidant properties and the seeds are highly nutritious.

Why is a **broad bean** seed often **included** in seventeenth century **Dutch** still life **paintings?**

They are a *memento mori*, a reminder of the souls of the dead who were believed to be contained within the beans and could, if necessary, ascend through the hollow stems. It was also believed that accidents were more likely to occur when the broad bean was in flower and, more bizarrely that it grew upside down during Leap Years. The good news is that if you scatter them around your house on New Year's Eve with the chant: 'With these beans I redeem me and mine'; the spirits of the dead will leave you in peace – no clambering up the hollow stems.

One of the other still life incidentals is often a walnut which symbolises the life and passion of Christ – the wood of the shell and the kernel of life within. Like so much Christian symbolism it is predated by the classical association with Jupiter because of the outer strength of the shell and the double inner shape associations of intelligence (brain like shape) and fertility (testicular arrangement) of the nut. The Latin name *Juglans* – Jove's glands – encapsulates this.

What do the **holly** and the **ivy** and the **oak** symbolise?

Evergreen and shiny, holly symbolises night whilst the great oak symbolises day which is why you see them depicted in historic tapestries and illustrations with the unicorn (night) and the lion (sun or day). The clinging ivy represents steadfastness and a signification of being clothed – hopefully with glory.

How can I use **broad beans** to know **what** the **future** holds?

First, gather three broad beans on Midsummer Eve: leave one intact; half-peel the second; and remove all the skin from the third. Next, ask someone to hide them and whichever one you find first is your destiny – wealth, a comfortable life or poverty.

What are the **origins** of broad **beans?**

Wild broad beans are the size of a little fingernail and they still grow, as they did tens of thousands of years ago, in south-eastern Afghanistan, Central Asia and the Himalayan foothills. Once ripe, they spread themselves about by rolling back their pods into a spiral and ejecting their seeds, but gatherers noticed that some never managed to open so they took them back to hull at home. This convenient packaging was selected for home cultivation and so the domestic broad bean evolved. In the 'Cave of the Spirit' in north-east Thailand, archaeological evidence has been found of two improved varieties being grown by the seventh millennium BC. In the cave of Taumalipas in Mexico broad beans dating back 7,000 years

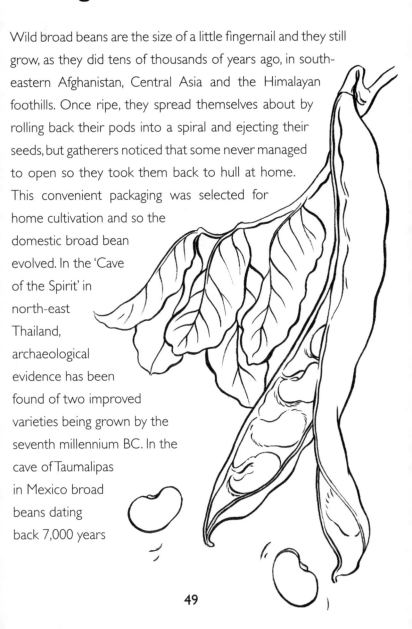

have been found. The Greeks even used broad beans as ballot papers. Ancient broad beans have a characteristic hilum (the scar on the seed at which the funicle or stalk was attached) at the apex of the bean seed which has enabled archaeologists working in Pompeii to identify them. Entomologists studying one ancient Roman bean at the Smithsonian extracted the hind legs of a strawberry weevil using tiny tweezers.

Which **medieval bean** has **become** a latter day **Christian** martyr?

The small brown seed of the Martock broad bean grew undisturbed for centuries in the gardens of the Bishops of Bath and Wells, too hard to eat green but an excellent source of winter protein after long slow cooking. Its second coming was as a result of its seeds being sold to help the restoration funds for Wells Cathedral. Too hard for many palates it has assumed a sacrificial role in organic gardens, it is a martyr to blackfly thus nobly attracting them away from the other plants.

Why are **pinks**, and later **carnations**, used to **decorate** the margins of **medieval** ecclesiastical illuminations?

They are symbolic of nails. Their scent wafts the spicy smell of cloves, cloves are the dried unopened flower buds of *Syzygium aromaticum* formerly known as *Caryophyllum*. The first name based on its botanical structure – *syn* – together, *zygon* – yoke because of the petal structure; the second *karya* – walnut and *phyllon* – leaf. The scent is similar to walnut leaves hence the old English synonym of gillyflowers. The common name for cloves derives from the Latin for nails – *clavus* – because that is what they look like. To carry the metaphor to its conclusion many Christian images allude to the passion of Jesus Christ nailed to a cross for their sake. The smell of cloves was also believed to drive away evil. The clove tree is something of a martyr as it is rarely allowed to show its brilliant red flowers and enjoy its other name of Zanzibar Red Head. It is mentioned in Chinese literature in the early years of 200 BC as being suitable for sweetening the breath before addressing the Emperor.

What makes the **Crown** Imperial, **Fritillaria** imperialis, cry but **never** shed a **tear** all the time it is in **flower?**

Look carefully up into the flowers at the top of each floret and you will see that each one has a teardrop clinging onto the petal grooves. Legend has it that the proud Crown Imperial was flowering as Christ walked through the garden, but unlike the other flowers she did not bow her head. Jesus turned and gently rebuked her for her haughty manners; ashamed and saddened, her petal grooves filled with tears that have never been dried.

Can **lettuces cool** passion?

The tomato may have blushed when it saw the salad dressing but lettuce would have taken the heat out of any steamy relationship. Apart from the soporific effects of its milky fluid, three versions of the sad end of Adonis and all passion spent for Venus have sealed the anaphrodisiac fate of the lettuce.

One recounts that Adonis was killed in a field of lettuce; another that Venus in her grief laid out the dead body of

Adonis on a bed of lettuce; finally that in her grief Venus threw herself onto a bed of lettuce in the hopes that its cooling properties would repress her desires and she would find calming comfort. With all these tears perhaps that's why lettuces are such martyrs to downy mildew and how appropriate that one of the most resistant strains is called Batavia Blonde. Should you, like Venus, wish to repress your desires, try tossing the seventeenth century Nicolas Culpeper's anaphrodisiac salad of lettuce, purslane, mint and vinegar.

Why are **rhinos** euphoric about **Euphorbia?**

Euphorbia helps to make the male rhinos of Namibia planning to woo absolutely irresistible to the female of the species. They straddle the large thornless Euphorbia in order to extract the sap by rubbing their genitalia across it until they are liberally coated in sap. One other unexpected result that can also be assumed is that that they do not suffer from warts, unlike King Juba of Mauretania whose physican Euphorbus burnt them off his hands with the caustic sap. On hearing this story, Dioscorides decided to name this African succulent plant Euphorbia. He called the Euphorbia grown by gardeners in Europe 'tithymalus' and further north 'esula'. Some 1,700 years later Linnaeus, the great classifier and observer of plant's sexual parts, counted the stamens, ovaries and ovules and widened the genus *Euphorbia* to include the African Euphorbia and European tithymalus and esula.

What is the difference between daffodils and narcissus?

The Latin name *Narcissus* applies to both and there are about fifty species, however, the common names are split: narcissus is used for daffodils with small cups like the Pheasant's Eye whilst daffodil is used for cultivars with trumpets or, correctly, coronas, such as King Alfred. According to the myth, Narcissus was a young man who fell in love with his own reflection in a pool. Longing to get closer to his own beauty he edged forward, fell into the water and drowned. Fortunately, the bulbs are better rooted so can be safely planted along the banks of streams and pools where we can enjoy their reflection in still water. Wordsworth's host of golden daffodils were drifts of the British naturalised daffodil, *N. pseudonarcissus*, better known as Lent lily because of its flowering period. Legend has it that the Romans introduced it into Britain as part of their *materia medica* but there are equally strong arguments that it is a native plant. Pliny wrote that Roman doctors used two varieties whose roots tasted like honey wine; they mixed the root with honey for burns and skin abrasions. The root of its name is *narke* meaning numbness or torpor because of its narcotic properties. The flowers were steeped in oil to soften callouses.

Which lotus is sacred?

The *Nelumbo nucifera*. Its first name is the Sinhalese for lotus and its second means nut bearing; its beauty was believed to be

near to perfection and the seeds are almost immortal. There are only two species of *Nelumbo* which grace still water with wax bloomed foliage and fragrant yellow, pink or white flowers that are held above the water like finely wrought chalices. Beautiful to the senses and good to eat, the leafstalks, root and seed are all edible. In warm sub-tropical countries the leafstalks can rise some 2.5m (8 ft) from the depths of the pool to the surface. Seeds that drop into the river mud can survive for several hundred years.

Homer's Lotus Eaters, the Lotophagi, feasted on another lotus – the *Zizyphus jujuba* whose name is derived from the Arabic *zizouf*. It is a small thorny deciduous tree that produces excellent dessert fruits that become sweeter if left to become spongy and wrinkled. Consuming these fruits induced the Lotophagi into a state of dreamy forgetfulness and stemmed the desire to return home. Apparently long term consumption also improves the complexion, so seek out and sample them using the modern common names of Jujube or Chinese date. The Chinese call the fruits 'big date' or *da zao* and the seeds *suan zao ren*, both of which are used in Chinese medicine not least in tandem with other medicines as a counter against side effects and literally to sweeten the pill. The fruits are prescribed for chronic fatigue, loss of appetite, diarrhoea, anaemia, irritability and hysteria. The seeds are used in cases of palpitations, insomnia, nervous exhaustion, night sweats and excessive perspiration.

Why is **mistletoe** so **legendary?**

Just the sight of its translucent white berries and pale green branches growing away from the soil, high up on the dormant bark of apple and oak trees exudes a defiance of nature. Its Breton name translates as Herb of the Cross because it was believed that the Cross was made from its once fine wood, and in punishment the magnificent tree was reduced to a parasite.

Mistletoe appears in Norse legend in the story of Balder the Good, the best and the brightest of the gods much beloved by Thor, his mother, Frigga, the other gods and all living creatures. Dreams warned Balder that he was in deadly peril, Frigga was determined to forestall any danger and forced all to swear never to hurt him. Fire, water, iron, stones, earths, diseases, beasts, birds, insects and poisons all took the oath except one tiny plant, the seemingly powerless mistletoe living courtesy of the oak tree.

All was jolly in the Norse wood except for one blind god, Hödur, who felt excluded from the merriment. The Dark Spirit, Loki, never one to lose an opportunity, appeared in their midst as a peasant woman and learned that the mistletoe was not bound to the oath. He fashioned a dart out of the mistletoe wood and urged Hödur to join in the games by trying his hand at throwing it. In innocent delight he threw aimlessly but the target proved to be Balder's heart; pierced, he fell dead to the ground and the mistletoe became the symbol of sacred power.

How did the Druids harvest for maximum potency?

The Druids believed mistletoe contained the potent life of its host the oak and would protect them from spirits as well as ensuring good luck and fecundity. On the sixth night of the moon, two white bulls were sacrificed as white robed Druids harvested the mistletoe. They pruned with golden sickles, dropping the branches into a white cloth so that they never touched the ground and did not lose their potency. Pliny extolled the virtues of mistletoe as a medicine for curing epilepsy and increasing women's fertility if cut during a new moon and not with an iron tool.

Whether you kiss or not under the Christmas bough of mistletoe you should take the branches down on Twelfth Night and keep the twigs to burn under the Christmas pudding. In the nineteenth century the bough was decorated, like a Christmas tree, with nuts, apples and ribbons.

Can you plant **mistletoe?**

Establishing mistletoe is notoriously difficult. First, the host tree needs to be at least twenty years old, and then the berries should be squashed against the host tree so that the seeds are rubbed into the bark, after which you hope for the best. In nature this is most efficiently done by birds as the berries have a sticky viscous quality which makes the birds wipe their bottoms against the bark leaving the seeds clean and stuck in place.

When is **an apple** not an **apple?**

In the Garden of Eden, Eve tempted Adam with a sweet luscious fruit, in Hebrew *tappauch*, a fruit that is better translated as a wild apricot. The golden apples of the Hesperides were probably pomegranates or even oranges. In English 'apple' was used as a good descriptive name for anything that is a fruit, thus tomatoes were introduced as love apple, dates eaten as finger apples, while the pineapple is a fruit with a shape like a pinecone, and on the other hand, the prickly fruit of the poisonous Datura is called a thorn apple.

Where did **dessert apples** originate?

Dessert apples originated in the Tian Shan forest on the borders of Kyrgyzstan and China where they evolved attractive fleshy fruits which were especially enjoyed by bears. The pulp was digested and, being gently laxative, the pips passed through free from pulp ready packaged for germination. Horses plying the trade routes into Europe also introduced ready packaged apple seedlings. Early farmers introduced this apple into Turkey around 6,500 BC and the Romans introduced them into Britain. The DNA of modern English apples is almost identical to that of those still growing in the Tian Shan forest.

The native crab apple was believed to have powers of love and fertility by the Celts, and it remains a useful pollinating apple in orchards today. One of the earliest varieties of English comestible apple was the medieval Costard which was marketed by costermongers.

Myth joins reality in the story of Johnny Appleseed who was born John Chapman in Leominster, Massachusetts and who is reputed to have raced across America scattering apple seeds. Romantic as it might seem this would not have guaranteed laden trees, the truth is more prosaic: from 1800 until his death in 1845 he established a string of nurseries distributing apple trees. He started in Pennsylvania, and headed west through Ohio and Indiana and north into New England. Finally, his apples were also exported to the West Indies.

Who **wept first**,
men or the
willows?

Man, who found a representative solace in the weeping willow which is a native of the Middle East. As Psalm 137 recalls 'By the rivers of Babylon, there we sat down, yea, we wept, when

we remembered Zion. We hanged our harps upon the willows in the midst thereof'. The native willows further north grew by wet places so all that water was inevitably associated with pools of tears. In England wearing a wreath or hat of willow showed that you had been rejected in love.

The weeping willow, *Salix Babylonica*, arrived in England around 1692. A delightful story sprang up that the poet Alexander Pope noticed some of the weave in a fig basket was still green so he teased it apart and tried to root the strands. The successfully rooted cutting grew into a weeping willow tree, so he was one of the first to grow, and indeed popularise the weeping willow, but not the introducer.

During the First World War as young men in France fought and died, the artist Claude Monet spent hours observing the twisted bark and weeping leaves of the willows in his garden at Giverny in Normandy. He painted them evocatively expressing the agony of Europe's grief. On a more practical note he sent boxes of fruit and vegetables from his gardens to the field hospitals nearby.

Is there a tartary lamb tree?

No, it is a fantastical plant that was featured on the front of John Parkinson's *Paradisi in Sole Paradisus Terrestris* in 1629. The legend was originally brought back by medieval travellers to Samarkand who reported that a vegetable lamb tree, known locally as Borametz, with feet, hooves, ears and a woolly head grew in far Tartary and Cathay. Travellers included men such as Geoffrey de Mandeville who claimed to have also spoken to people who had visited the Garden of Eden! Parkinson described the Tartary Lamb as a plant resembling a lamb attached by its navel to a stem three feet high and grown from a seed similar to that of a melon but 'lesse and longer'. Its head hung down so that it could graze, the woolly tufts from its head were woven into fabrics. The myth persisted and in 1656 the Tradescant Museum, whose collections formed the core of the Ashmolean Museum, listed 'a very small part' of a borametz skin and a coat lined with it.

Why do you serve mint sauce with lamb?

Sheep grazed water mint on the Romsey Marshes in Kent so it was said that their flesh had a pleasing mint flavour which was enhanced by being served with mint sauce. The best mint sauce is actually made of garden rather than water mint. The flesh of Welsh lamb was equally flavoured by the wild thyme that it grazed on the mountainsides so was cooked with sprigs of thyme.

Is it **unlucky** to bring **lilac** into the **house?**

Traditionally it was believed that if flowering lilac was taken into the house, misfortune would befall the inhabitants. What is a nuisance is that lilacs drop their petals everywhere.

What can **lilac** foretell?

In 1909 M. Trevelyan published *Folk-lore and Folk-stories of Wales* in which he wrote that lilac blossoms were supposed to indicate changes in the weather. If they stayed closed longer than usual, fine weather might be expected. If they opened rapidly, rain would fall soon. If the lilacs quickly droop and fade, a warm summer will follow. Late flowering lilacs indicate a rainy season. They are also a symbol of young love disappointed – look at the floor of the arbour scattered with lilac petals in Arthur Hughes' *April Love*: who has rejected who?

Are there any other **plants** I ought **not to** bring into the **house?**

Tradition also advises against bringing Forsythia, Hawthorn and Snowdrop into the house: the latter was believed to use the devil's power to push through the frozen ground. Witches are said to metamorphose into elder trees, *Sambucus*, and will bleed if cut down and under no circumstances should be used on open fires or in the house.

Which **wood** makes the **best witch's** broomstick?

'Witches Broom' is an excrescence on the Scot's Pine caused by the fungus *Pridermium elatinum*, which manifests itself in a multitude of short shoots, unpleasant for the tree but not a reliable witch-mobile. Witches took flights of fantasy on brooms, branches, beasts and flying carpets, but, as Erica Jong argues, it is not the vehicle but the metaphor of flight which expresses freedom and sexuality. Recipes for ointments countering a fear of flying abound, mixing lethal, hallucinogenic, fragrant and bizarre ingredients such as aconite, deadly nightshade, hemlock, cinquefoil, sweet flag, poplar leaves and parsley stirred up with soot and bats' blood. To speed up their effects they were often applied on a dildo – a broomstick by another name? In *The Witches Song* Ben Jonson includes the fairly standard ingredients of horned poppy, Cypress boughs, larch tree juice, and the slightly more esoteric wild fig-tree which grows on tombs. However, in order for the orgies to begin, he adds the distinctly unobtainable basilisk's blood and viper's skin.

How did the **horned poppy** get its name?

Simply because its long curved fruits appear simultaneously with the flowers but its Latin name *Glaucium* has more magical associations. Glaucus was a fisherman who noticed that no sooner had he laid out his catch on the coastal plants than they were revived and leapt back into the sea. He decided to test out the powers of the plants and when he nibbled the leaves of the horned poppy he was overcome with the desire to leap into the sea. In recognition of this Oceanus and Telhyst made him a sea god, today his image survives as one of the statues at Bomarzo in Italy. The leaves are edible and rich in iodine.

Where can you obtain **Dragon's** Blood?

On the Island of Socotra off the coast of the Yemen and in Somalia. It is extracted from the berries of the *Dracaena cinnabari* which is actually a vibrant red resin more excitingly termed Dragon's Blood.

Why do foxes wear **gloves?**

In Ireland fairies are believed to protect foxes and there is a legend that says foxes become invisible when they wear the flowers of the foxglove on their ears. Seedsmen Thompson and Morgan have recently introduced a new cultivar called 'Candy Mountain' with upward turned flowers so that we poor mortals can gaze down their speckled throats, but how are the foxes supposed to fit them on their ears?

Which plant is **associated** with **war** and the **Roman god** Mars?

Garlic, and Mars was the god of war. Roman soldiers carried garlic bulbs on campaign as part of their *materia medica*, eating

garlic was believed to strengthen both the body and the mind for war and love. The genus name for the onion family, *Allium*, derives from the classical name for garlic, its own binomial *A. sativum* means 'an onion cultivated by man'. The name 'gar leac' is derived from the Celtic meaning strong leek.

The characteristic smell of all alliums comes from the sulphur compounds which have such a beneficial effect on the digestive, respiratory and circulatory systems. Garlic is the greatest warrior in this fight, its antithrombotic activity is due to the ability of fresh extracts to inhibit platelet aggregation thus reducing the risk of forming blood clots – its active agents are ajoene and 2-vinyl-4H-1, 3-dithiin. In Ayuvedic medicine it is used as a rejuvenative, detoxicant and aphrodisiac. Planting garlic, or indeed any more ornamental alliums among your roses deters their predators as well as traditionally keeping vampires at bay.

A family of emotions in the rose bed – Mars, the god of war was consort to Venus the goddess of love and all growing things especially associated with roses, myrtle and apples. The fruit of their loins was Cupid who wooed Psyche, and their love blossomed into Pleasure which leads you down the Primrose Path.

3

Extreme Plants and Record Breakers

Could **Jack** have climbed **a beanstalk?**

Yes, if we forget the beanstalks that provide us with broad, green, runner, kidney and lima beans. If we take beans to mean a member of the legume family then Jack could have scaled the record holding stalks of *Entada scandens* or its close relative, *E. gigas*. *E. scandens* grows to a height of 140 metres with the world's longest known stems. Imagine the powerful internal pumping system it has in order to get water and nutrients from the tip of the roots to the topmost leaves. Apart from climbing into the unknown, if Jack had been thirsty, or should you ever find yourself lost in the jungle, if a stem is cut, the internal pump literally sprinkles water.

Jack might well have swapped his mother's cow for the impressive seeds of the *Entada*. The pods are 1.5m long and 10cm wide, made of a flat, hard and grey wood. There are up to fifteen glossy brown seeds which are about 6cm in diameter, which can be used to make attractive bracelets and ornaments. The wooden pods are buoyant and are washed up on European Atlantic coastlines. The pods of *E.gigas* contain what is called the Matchbox bean, a name dating back to the days of wax matches which were ignited on its rough outer seed coat. The outer coat gets very hot under friction, a point not missed by mischievous small boys in the past who used it to burn each other.

In Australia, the *E. phaseoloides,* or Matchbox bean, is native of the Queensland rain forests, and has the more modest height of 15 metres spreading to 100 metres. It has large trifoliate leaves and white pea-like flowers that ripen into pods of 1m long containing dark brown seeds that are 10cm long. When they were fishing, Aborigines used the seeds as a fish poison. They also crushed the seeds as a contraceptive; however, in order to be effective after ingestion apparently women had to lie down all day. The Coastal Jack Bean, *Convalia rosea,* is another sub tropical bean whose benign appearance belied its nature. Sailors thought they had found food in the bean like seeds, but they are poisonous, causing violent illness and vomiting.

How many plants are there?

There are over 400,000 species of plants of which *c.* 150,000 never produce flowers, and *c.* 150,000 grow from spores instead of seeds, while one third of plants have neither roots, stems nor leaves. There are 250,000 varieties available to agriculture of which less than three per cent are in use today – a resource monitored by crop breeders.

Where is the **greatest diversity** of plants?

Arguably, the greatest diversity can be found in the Cape Region on the south-west tip of Africa, where the score is currently running at 9,000 species. Seventy per cent of these are endemic, in 35,000 square miles, with more being discovered every year. Its unique vegetation is known as *fynbos*. The diversity of plants is matched by the variety of micro-habitats, coast to mountain, and soils, sandstone, shale and limestone. In a flora rich habitat like this, introduced flower species are often invasive, to the detriment of the fine ecological balance.

Pollination is ably assisted by dozens of different long-tongued flies. There are irises, orchids and geraniums completely dependent on the record-breaking probiscus of the giant nosed fly, *Moegistorhynchus longirostris*. Although these flowers are completely different species, they have evolved similarly structured flowers of small cream to salmon coloured petals poised on narrow, long tubes that hold a pool of nectar at their base. Only the *M. longirostris* has a long enough tongue, so it gets the nectar and each plant drops its pollen on a different part of its body. So while the tongue travels the distance, the plants match up individually by carefully positioning pollen, some on its head, others to its underside or its thorax and abdomen.

Which is the **world's largest** unbroken **forest?**

Not the Amazon but the Siberian Taiga or coniferous forest, whose vastness permits populations of large predators to interact naturally with their prey – not so good for the prey! There is a network of wetlands within it which provide a critical breeding habitat for many species of waterfowl, shorebirds and the endangered Siberian crane.

Which **continent** has the most **undisturbed** land?

In percentage terms based on sheer size the most undisturbed land can be found in the icy wastes of Antarctica but in planted earth terms South America. South America has the biologically rich Amazonian forests, and long may they survive; under the pressure of an annual estimated 18,000 square miles being cleared and levelled by farmers and commercial loggers, the threat is serious.

Where is the **largest stretch** of protected **rainforest** on Earth?

Now known as the Guyana Shield, it is in the state of Para in Brazil and extends to 15 million hectares. It is a legally protected zone guarded by satellite cameras and the 'conservation stewardship' of local tribes. It is estimated that it supports about fifty-four per cent of all Amazonian animal and plant species.

What is the **oldest green** life form?

The microscopic algae, fungi and bacteria that are always cold, hungry and cling to life inside rocks on Antarctica are thousands of years old but undated. They form the most primitive or first of the four plant divisions: Division one – the Thallophyta. The other three divisions are in order of evolutionary sophistication: Division two being the Bryophyta which have leaves and stems but no roots, and include mosses and liverworts. Division three is the Pteridophyta which have leaves, stems and roots, and include ferns, horsetails and clubmosses. Division four is the Spermatophyta, the top league of plant life, which represents the highest evolutionary progress, it is divided into gymnosperms and angiosperms (see p.3).

Which **tree** is both a **fossil** and **one** of the **latest** discoveries in the **world?**

The Wollemi pine, *Wollemia nobilis*, was growing some two hundred million years ago and was believed to have been extinct for the last two million years. Its original range probably encompassed eastern Australia, Antarctica, New Zealand and possibly India and southern South America. It emerged from the mists of time in September 1994, deep in the Wollemi National Park in the Blue Mountains 200 km from Sydney. Wollemi is an Aboriginal word meaning 'look around you, keep your eyes open and watch out' which is exactly what its discoverer, David Noble, was doing as he canyoned through its rugged wilderness.

At this time there are only one hundred mature trees known to man all growing in this one stand. It is a majestic conifer that grows to heights of 40 metres with a trunk diameter of over one metre, the mature bark looks like bubbling chocolate. Many have multiple trunks which have probably evolved as a survival adaptation against the drought, fire and rock fall that are the ever present dangers of growing in these steep canyons. The unusual pendulous foliage has light apple-green new tips in spring and early summer which contrast against the older dark blue-green foliage. One unique feature is its 'polar caps' which are formed from the wax coating which appears in the winter to protect the new growing tips – the original snow effects tree?

This dinosaur tree can now be seen in a botanical garden or park near you; cuttings have been taken, rooted and distributed worldwide. The good news is that this is also a project open to anyone prepared to pay and plant. The hardy Wollemi Pine ticks all the ornamental boxes including hard pruning, it does not have needle drop and can be trained as a bonsai. It is not a pine but in the monkey puzzle tree family, *Araucariaceae*, a new puzzle that looks set to leave rarity behind and reforest the world.

How old, where and **what** is the **oldest** tree in **the world?**

Reputedly 11,700 years old, the Creosote Plant, *Larrea tridentata*, holds the record. Its common name recalls that its sap is treated at high temperatures to produce creosote. The slowest growing record holder is a Bristlecone pine, *Pinus aristata*, which has passed its 4,900th birthday, having been dated back to 2,926 BC. Its longevity is aided by its wood being saturated in resin.

Another contender of enormous religious importance is the Sacred Bo Tree, *Sri Maha Bodhi*, in Sri Lanka which is a sapling from the original tree under which the Buddha attained enlightenment in Bodhi Gaya in India. It was brought to Sri Lanka 2,300 years ago and planted in Anuradhapura where it still grows. Seedlings from this tree have been planted in Buddhist temples in Sri Lanka and beyond, especially in Japan.

In 1998 elevated sea levels washed away the sands along a 185 mile strip of the Oregon coastline in the United States exposing an ancient forest floor known as the Neskowin stumps. These four hundred or more stumps range in size up to six feet in diameter, they were probably about two hundred years old when felled 1,700 to 2,000 years ago. Earlier storms have exposed ancient stumps that date back 4,000 years.

Can plants **survive without** rain?

On the so-called Skeleton Coast of Namibia in south-west Africa the aridity makes life of any kind almost impossible. One ground hugging tree that has adapted to the drought is the *Weiwilschia mirabilis* which takes its moisture from the fogs. From a hard core it sends out very battered long flat side leaves that can catch the dew and drain any moisture back to the core.

What is the
most **expensive**
plant in the world?

In recent history possibly the Hyacinth 'Midnight Mystique' which was officially offered to the gardening public in March 2005.

Seven years earlier the seed company Thompson and Morgan had bought just three bulbs for £150,000 from which they managed to raise 28,000 by scooping rather than through tissue culture. Scooping is so called because a specialised spoon with a sharp edge is used for this form of propagation. A hyacinth bulb has a basal plate from which the roots grow, a central shoot that supports the flower, and around the central shoot are scale leaves – looking as they sound; all of these have the potential to form bulblets and root. Expert propagators remove the basal plate and the central shoot, then using the spoon, scoop out a concave depression from the base that exposes the base of the scale leaves. The scale leaves then go into overdrive producing new bulblets. Cut too deep and you destroy the scale leaves potential, cut too shallow and any parts of the basal plate left will inhibit new bulblets. The new bulbs retailed at £8 each.

As the name suggests, the flowers are virtually black. It certainly would be mysterious at midnight as black flowers recede

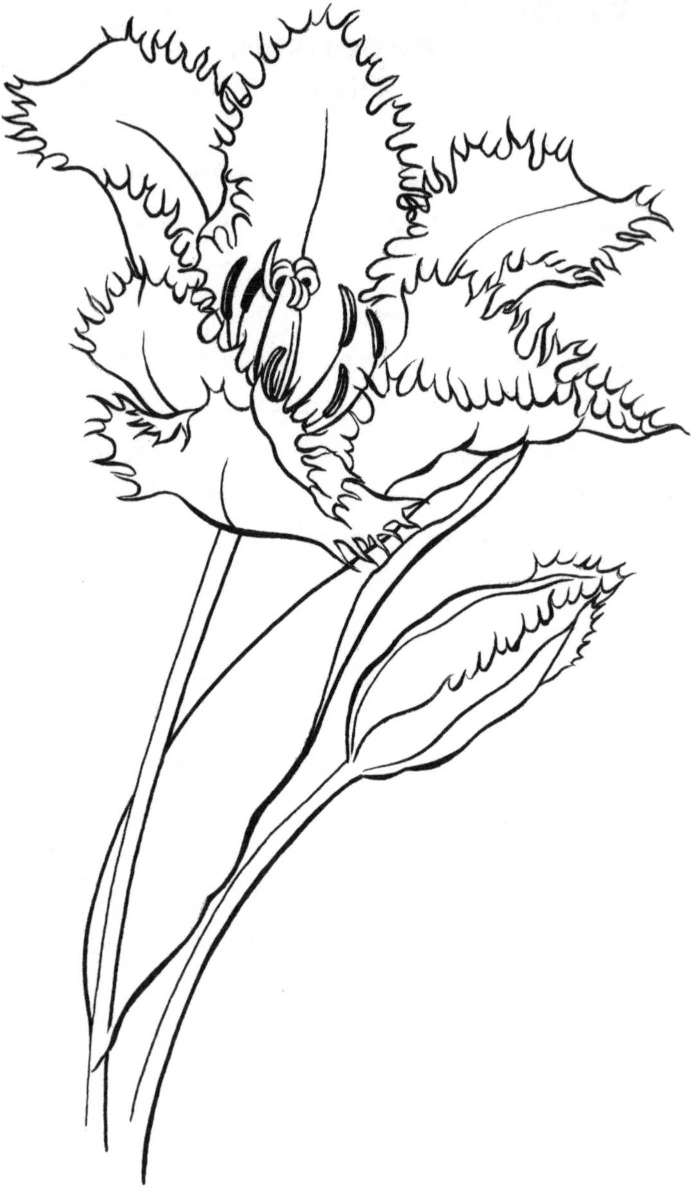

into the background leaving their paler luminous colleagues to make a show. The mystique of black flowers and human greed to create them is recounted in dramatic fashion by Alexandre Dumas in *The Black Tulip* but it was not until 1937 that Tulip 'Black Parrot' was produced, followed by 'Queen of the Night' in 1944 and 'Black Swan' in 1963. Black is sought after as rare and exotic as well as having desirable qualities such as the velvet-like flowers of Iris chrysographes 'The Black Night'. Latin specific epithets help in the quest for black: *niger, nigra* and *nigrum* usually refer to the roots. For black leaves look out for *nigratus, nigrata, nigratum, Nigrescens, nigrans,* if you want healthy black spots then check out *nigropunctatus, nigropunctata* and *nigropunctatum.*

The Bat Plant, *Tacca chantrierei,* echoes its name with dusky black blooms with bat like tentacles extending to 30cm (12in). Jack in the Pulpit is a common name applied to several plants (see Mating and Dating p.165) but in its incarnation as *Arisaema sikokianum,* it is black with a striking white throat and spadix, perhaps he could clear his throat to warn his congregation about the Black Witch's Broom, *Sorghum nigrum.* On a sadder note Scabious 'Ebony and Ivory' means 'I have lost all', as its colours nearly replicate the colour of a widow's weeds with tiny white anthers as a bouquet for the lost one. In Devon it is called Mournful Widow and in France the Widow's Flower.

Ebony, *Diospyros,* wood is dense, fine-grained and hard, and amongst other uses, is made into the black keys on a piano.

The *Diospyros* family also includes the Persimmon whose wood is also dense, fine-grained and hard but creamy white and used for golf club heads.

Why are the **plants** in **Hawaii** defenceless **natives?**

Hawaii has no indigenous browsing animals so the native flora did not need the usual defence systems of thorns or toxins. Attack has come from two fronts: introduced domestic animals that have browsed and caused untold damage; and introduced plants that have naturalised, to compete with and sometimes overrun native plants.

What are **the oldest** viable **seeds?**

Those of the Arctic Lupin, *Lupinus archticites*, which like many seeds after chilling, waits for warmth to break out of its dormancy. A native of the Arctic Tundra, the seeds get blown into protective crevices that will provide a foothold if they germinate. If they fail in the first year, debris accumulates above them and freezes; once this reaches a few inches it becomes part of the permafrost. In what is described as 'nature's deep freeze', the seeds remain viable for tens of thousands of years. Modern scientists have excavated such examples and have managed to germinate a low percentage

Japanese gardens celebrate the arrival of each blossom and flower, but none more so than one seed found in an archaeological site dating back two thousand years to the Yayoi period. Amongst the shrivelled grains of rice they found one seed which miraculously germinated, and was identified as the wild *Magnolia kobus*. Eleven years later it flowered but in a form never seen before: as the petals unfurled there were eight rather than six, in the following years, the number of flowers ranged from six to nine. Untouched, indeed untainted, by two thousand years of cross pollination, this magnolia is a living witness to genetic evolution.

What is the **highest** tree?

The record is held by the appropriately named giant redwood, *Sequoiadendron giganteum*. In 2006 Humboldt State University found the latest record breaker in California's Redwood National Park, coming in at the massive height of 115m. In 1853 the English plant hunter, William Lobb, happened to attend a meeting of the Californian Academy of Science who had invited a hunter to retell his adventures in the foothills of the Sierra

Nevada in Calaveras County. The hunter had stumbled into a grove of mammoth trees so tall that he could only marvel. Lobb raced to see what he later described as the 'Monarch of the Californian forest' and secure seeds; he noted that he had found eighty or ninety trees within a mile that were 250 to 320ft in height and 10 to 20ft in diameter. Mission completed, he took the first ship home from San Francisco. His employers, Veitch's Nurseries, were ecstatic and set about raising plants

In England it was decided that so magnificent a tree should be named for the Iron Duke – *Wellingtonia*; American botanists reacted rapidly – why should an American plant be named by the British for their hero, why not theirs and call it *Washingtonia*? The nomenclature soil was raked and a compromise was planted, *Sequoia* for the indigenous Indian tribe (*dendron* literally means tree) and its close relative the Coastal Redwood, *Sequoia sempervirens*, whilst *giganteum* speaks for itself.

Sadly while this international dispute raged tourists flocked for the Great Tree experience, an exercise in wanton damage – a dance floor was set up across the felled trunk of another and a bowling alley through another. In more recent history, I can remember one of my childhood encyclopaedias depicting a car driving through the centre. Somewhat appropriately, the largest specimen has now been named 'General Sherman' and Calaveras Grove is now protected by a National Park.

One of Lobb's earlier finds was the Monterey pine, *Pinus radiata*. Found nowhere on earth except the Monterey peninsula its seeds were left by the retreating glaciers after the

Ice Age. In North America the north/south mountain ranges created linear dropping pockets, in Europe the Alps stopped plants travelling further north.

What are the shortest and longest living flowers?

Judgment is easiest if you assess this on the lifespan of the flower's petals, so the answer is orchids in Malaysia. Petals usually only live until the flower is pollinated and having served their attractant purpose die – so lasting just five minutes are the petals of the orchid *Dendrobium appendicultum,* which all open simultaneously for mass pollination. On the other hand *Grammatophyllum multiflorum* lasts a leisurely nine months.

Which plant needs a record breaking moth?

In Madagascar there is an orchid, *Angraecum sesquipedale,* whose nectary is 21-30cm down the flower spur. On seeing this, Charles Darwin observed that somewhere in Madagascar there would be a pollinator with a tongue to match. Forty years later a hawk moth, *Xanthopan morgani-praedicta,* was discovered with a probiscus of up to 22½ cm which is kept

rolled up like a coil when not in use. The names of orchid and pollinator encapsulate the story – *sesquipedale* – one and a half feet; *praedicta* – the one that was predicted.

Many flowers such as honeysuckles and capers are especially shaped for Hawk moths to pollinate. Hawk moths hover while inserting their long probiscus which makes dusting them with pollen difficult. Lady's Fingers is an old name for Honeysuckle, and their long elegance draws the hawk moth in sufficiently that he receives a good pollen powdering. The caper has adapted by separating the stamens, ovary and stigma in the flower; the stigma stands proud like a baton, the stamens fall all around the petals and the nectary lies right at the bottom of the flower so a clean swoop by the pollinator is impossible.

Can **plants spit** their **seeds** as far as **man** can spit **cherry** stones?

If seeds are spat across land the measurement is straightforward and humans would be the winners but many plants use intermediaries. Sometimes seeds are ejected onto a passing animal, into a stream, into the sea, or are so light that they waft up into space. The pollen from wind pollinated plants can end up 19,000ft into the sky and 3,000 miles away across the earth. Downy Dandelion seeds aim for the sky and into space where their featherweight parachutes have been found floating in the lowest strata of the atmosphere, the troposphere. Buoyant seeds can be washed up thousands of miles away from the parent plant.

One Broom, *Sarothamnus scoparius*, explodes once as a flower and then again as a pod. The flowers have to fine tune the timing of their pollen explosion as it can only happen once because the stigma must be simultaneously mature. It is triggered by the visit of either a bumble or honey bee, which on landing makes the flower sink in turn making the keel open explosively. Later, in the August sun, the pods turn black as they ripen so increasing the rate of absorbing the heat and drying out. At the right moment of desiccation they explode by rolling up into a spiral and firing the seeds several metres. The final distance is achieved by ants that drag them away to enjoy the greasy compound surrounding the seeds. Once satisfied they leave the seeds to germinate.

The bristly Squirting Cucumber, *Ecballium elaterium*, develops a beer belly filled with juicy pulp corked by its stopper like stalk. When it can contain itself no longer, it breaks away from its stalk and automatically squirts its seeds uncontrollably.

Does **bread** grow on **trees?**

Yes, when it is a breadfruit. It is a record-breaker in the utility feeding stakes with a mass of sweet, starchy, seedless pulp which when roasted in its thick skin achieves the consistency and taste of fresh bread. A variety, the Jack Fruit, *Artocarpus heterophyllus* and closely related to the breadfruit, *Artocarpus communis*, is both the biggest edible fruit and instigator of the Mutiny on the Bounty. The Jack Fruit weighs in at 25kg and can be 90cm long.

In 1787 Sir Joseph Banks commissioned *HMS Bounty* to set sail for the South Seas with the task of transporting breadfruit plants from Tahiti's Society Islands across to feed the plantation slaves on the Caribbean island of Jamaica. The ship was fitted out to carry hundreds of pots of breadfruit trees, tenderly protected from the salt water by a cabin greenhouse. In order to irrigate these precious trees Captain William Bligh rationed his crew's drinking water which drove them to mutiny. They dumped him and other members of the crew, leaving them defenceless, adrift on the Pacific Ocean for forty-seven days – the rest is history. However, in 1793 Bligh returned on *HMS Providence*, collected breadfruit trees and delivered them to the Caribbean islands – where bread still grows on trees.

Which is the largest leaf?

Impress your friends and find a Giant Taro, *Alocasia macrorrhiza*, which has the largest undivided leaf. It is also known as the Elephant's-Ear Plant, and can reach 3m across. It is pollinated by snails which slide in through a narrow opening in the spathe and wander helplessly around dusting themselves with pollen which is then conveniently conveyed to the stigmas. Not just a big leaf, it also has edible roots and is closely related to *Colocasia* whose roots yield the cocoyam and eddo. The crowd puller leaf has to be that of the giant water lily, *Victoria amazonica*, which can attain a diameter of over two metres (six feet). Its daily growth is prodigious and at its peak can attain an overall gain of four to five square feet in twenty-four hours. The deep- ribbed structure of the under surface of the mammoth leaf is such that its network forms small pockets of air like buoyancy aids between the upper leaf and water surfaces.

Who first got Victoria to flower?

The Head Gardener at Chatsworth in Derbyshire, Joseph Paxton, was the first to coax the giant water lily into flower, beating Kew. On 17 November 1849 *The Illustrated London News* published an engraving of Paxton's seven-year-old daughter Annie dressed as a fairy standing on a leaf to demonstrate its strength. Since then the weight-bearing abilities of the leaf have been more critically tested, the leaf has sustained an

11st man on a flat board for two minutes. The structure of the leaf inspired Paxton's most famous design, the 1851 Great Exhibition Hall, better known as The Crystal Palace. Paxton observed 'Nature has provided the leaf with longitudinal and transverse girders and supports that I, borrowing from it, have adopted in this building.'

The flowers are equally a crowd puller, a floral equivalent of a matinee and evening performance of Swan Lake rolled into one. At 2pm the white bud begins to emit a fruity scent, over the next two to three hours the petals unfurl and deepen in colour, by ten o'clock they close. The following day the dying flower descends gracefully back into the water. Although named for Queen Victoria during her lifetime the giant water lily was called *Victoria regia* as joining the dear queen's name with *amazonica* was felt to be inappropriate.

Which is the **most effective** weed?

Poor environment and upbringing makes plants become survivors and opportunists. Apart from the definition that a weed is a plant in the wrong place, weeds come in two types: ruderals are the weeds that colonise waste and disturbed ground while agrestals compete with crops in cultivated ground. One agrestal that is Arabis-like in appearance but weed-like in action is the rapid seeding thale cress, *Arabidopsis thaliana*, that produces eight generations a year. A cultivator's nightmare but a geneticist's dream, these quickfire generations allow scientist to quickly track evolutionary changes.

Can it be **true** that the **biggest flower** in the **world** has no leaves, **stem** or root?

Yes, the 1 m wide flowering *Rafflesia arnoldii* is just an oversized parasite and is a splendid illustration of this Greek word that means to eat at other men's tables. It starts life as a slimy pulp filled with developing seeds, and its distribution is aided by the digestive systems of elephants and other animals. In a nine month gestation period the seeds penetrate the roots of a species of vine, the *Cissus,* and develop covertly in the host tissue until they rupture the bark like small cabbages. The nectarium that forms at the centre of the flower can hold several gallons of liquid, the five petals which can be up 1cm thick are a brilliant red with dirty white patches. Awesome but unattractive, just to top the whole experience off, it exudes a foul stench of carrion. This stench attracts the pollinator as well as human seekers of sexual stimulants and fertility charms. It is named for its intrepid discoverers, the English diplomat, Sir Stamford Raffles and American naturalist, Dr. Joseph Arnold, when they were exploring in the interior of Sumatra.

What makes **chilli peppers** so **hot?**

They contain a chemical called capsaicin which activates a nerve cell receptor called TRPV1, which triggers the same pain reaction as the bite of a Trinidad chevron tarantula. The heat is a defence mechanism in that it is anti-microbial, therefore, stopping rotting. They have been used to punish promiscuity

– anyone chopping fresh chilli peppers knows not to touch their eyes or any other sensitive part of their anatomy.

What is the most **extreme** nettle?

The great Shrubby Nettle, *Urtica crenulata*, known in its native Himalayas as *mealum-ma* grows up to 5m (15ft) high. It has broad glossy leaves and can strike in two ways. The worst attacks are in the autumn when it has a virulent sting. It is the microscopically small hairs on the nettles that inflict an initial slight pricking, slowly but steadily a burning pain spreads into the body peaking in agony and the jaws locking. Over the next nine days the torture slowly subsides. The other way it attacks during the year is by tainting the air with a scentless effluvium which makes the eyes and nose pour with mucous.

Victorian travellers' tales about Java speak of another nettle, *Urtica stimulans,* being rubbed on to buffaloes to incite them to fight tigers. There are some seriously ferocious stingers in Tropical Australia: the Gympic Bush, *Dendrocride moroides*, the Stinging Tree, *D. codata*, rising to 15m, the Great Stinging Tree, *D. excelsa* and last, but not least, the Mulberry leafed stinging tree, *D. photiniphylla.*

Which **weed**
ate the **South**
USA?

A Japanese plant called Kudzu, *Pueraria lobata* which can grow up to 30cm (1ft) a day in summer and 30m (100ft) in a season while sending down roots 2m (6ft) and more. It made its first appearance in the United States at the 1876 Philadelphia Centennial Exposition in the Japanese Pavilion. In the 1930s and 1940s the American government promoted it as the 'mile-a-minute vine' that would stem soil erosion from the depleted cotton fields. In 1936 farmers were paid $8 for every acre planted with kudzu and by 1943 the Atlanta-based Kudzu Club of America boasted 20,000 members. Today it has overrun abandoned houses, smothered trees and just keeps climbing its way through Maryland and tidewater Virginia, into the Ohio River Valley, then east to Texas and Oklahoma where it now blankets millions of acres.

Can **anyone**
or anything **bring kudzu**
under control?

Crafts people in the south eastern USA weave the vines into baskets and wreaths, goats graze it reasonably effectively but not enough. In fact enough to drive you to drink, unless Americans follow the Japanese example and start using it as an ancient herbal remedy for alcoholism – modern research has isolated two chemicals didzain and daidzein which reduce the craving for alcohol. It also has a host of culinary uses: the roots can be steamed or boiled like potatoes, and when dried into a powder it is an excellent thickener. The young tender parts can be eaten in salads, sautéed and casseroled. So the South needs to eat the weed before it eats them.

What **other plants** are **thugs?**

Florida already spends $11 million each year trying to control the water hyacinth which was introduced in the 1880s – they also ought to try eating the flowers as they are delicious in salad. The Chinese guava tree has similarly blanketed and killed the endemic indigenous flora of Mauritius. The tree *Miconia* is called a green cancer in Hawaii where it has overrun 20,000 acres in the last forty years.

Which **plant** **is most** eaten in the **world?**

Rice, which was first cultivated in Thailand c. 6000 BC. It grows wild in southern China and in the Yangtze delta where there is evidence of rice paddies or wet rice production dating back to 5,000 BC. Today production exceeds 350 metric tonnes annually, let alone all the little domestic patches. It is the staple diet for over half the world's population.

4

Mating and Dating

Why is an **alga** like a **human?**

An alga with a name longer than itself, *Clamydomonas reinhardtii*, has two specialised reproductive cells called gametes, which mate to form a unique individual with a mixture of genetic material from both parents. Under a microscope their methods and their gametes look amazingly similar to a human sperm fertilising a human egg.

Do plants reproduce themselves **sexually?**

Yes, in two ways: either male and female on one plant, or separate male and female plants. They are termed monoecious when they have functional male stamens and functional female pistils on the same plant and so can self pollinate. An example of this is the newly discovered dinosaur tree, Wollemi Pine, which has long male cones that produce the pollen, and round female cones that produce seeds on the same tree, (see p. 78) They are called dioecious when they have unisexual flowers on different plants; one plant is staminate or male – bearing stamens but no functional pistils; the other plant is pistillate or female, so she can draw her pistils but has not functional stamens.

What are **particles** of **prolific** value?

In general terms they are the pollen which must be transmitted to the stigma as prolifically as possible by insects, birds, bats, passing mammals; or the wind, or water, for fertilisation. For man their value lies in the resultant bumper harvests of bread, fruit and vegetables.

Who else **profits** from **pollen?**

Insects are efficient and waste little pollen, but they get the best value from entomophilous pollen that has evolved on plants that attract them by colour, odour and/or nectar. Insect pollinated plants offer quality rather than quantity; pollen is usually available at less than 10,000 grains per anther. We should develop a bee in our bonnet about safeguarding bee habitats, as directly and indirectly their busy pollination provides every third mouthful of our food.

If you are an archaeologist using palynology (pollen analysis) the profligacy of anemophilous pollen is invaluable, it is found on wind pollinated plants and trees such as pine trees, where an average tree produces some 350 million pollen grains. Anemophilous pollen floats around attaching itself to animal fur or droppings, often ending up in middens unused and unfulfilled for its proper purpose, but providing archaeological evidence of flora, fauna, diet and climate change thousands of years later.

In the human-dominated vegetation of Europe, pollen analysis has helped to identify the original flora long since replaced by agriculture and horticulture.

What are
stamens?

These are a flower's male organs where you will find the pollen: they are composed within the filament which holds a container with four compartments at its tip. This is known as the anther and is where you see the pollen. In the eighteenth and nineteenth centuries, the stamens in lilies were considered so shockingly erect that they were removed when used for flower arranging. Today they are removed in case they stain clothes and tablecloths.

As winter warms into early spring, the male catkins on the hazel, *Corylus avellana*, extend into flower, each consisting of four cleft stamens making eight anthers. Each flowering catkin is made up of about a thousand anthers, and together they produce two and a half million anemophilous pollen grains which are distributed by buffetings from rough winds.

What is a **pistil?**

The flower's discreet female organs: the pistil consists of a stigma, style and ovary. You could say that there is no stigma in having style and certainly no danger looking down the barrel of this pistil. The stigma has utility not beauty, in order to receive and hold desirable pollen for the ovary, or seed box, to do its work of fertilisation, the stigma is sticky and glutinous often with the additions of warts and hairs. The style usually connects the stigma and the seed box. The stigma only sticks to useful pollen, undesirable alien pollen is rejected by secretions that inhibit fertilisation.

Which plant has been **trying** to **date** for over **one hundred** years?

A cycad, *Encephalartos woodii*, which is the sole survivor of the species, a male, remains in Natal in South Africa. It is about 5ft tall with leathery leaves. This last surviving wild plant has been moved and cuttings taken, but as a dioecious species i.e. it has separate male and female species, he can never produce naturally until a female is found.

Are **flowers** bisexual?

Most seed plants have bisexual flowers; just think of the convenience and efficiency of developing fruit in-house. The following two trees provide examples of mix and match sexual and bisexual methods. Conkers from Horse chestnuts, *Aesculus hippocastanum,* are the products of male and bisexual flowers on the same inflorescence. In the Ash, all variations are unlocked by Ash keys, the winged seeds of *Fraxinus excelsior,* which are produced by male, female and bisexual flowers.

Which **plants** are **shamelessly** alluring and **overt?**

There is the teasing bee orchid, *Ophrys apifera*, whose scent mirrors that of the female bumblebee ready for a little light intercourse. The hapless drone drifts in on the luring wafts and to his delight sees a welcoming brown furry abdomen seductively framed in the pink sepals and green flower petals. A moment not to be wasted, he is fired into action, he sinks his head into the blossom and rubs his body against her ready for pleasurable penetration. No such luck, his increasingly jerky movements fail to achieve coition, horror of horrors, he then thinks he is in competition with another male whose apparent scent and aggressive squeezings surround him. Frustrated he breaks free having only succeeded in covering himself with a heavy powdering of yellow pollen. As he comes up for air he detects the unmistakeable scent of another willing female and with determination heads off in her direction – for a similarly frustrating experience for him but not for the moist stamens that snatch his plentiful supply of pollen to initiate fertilisation. There is nothing promiscuous in the bee orchid's behaviour, she has evolved to attract only bumblebees and mirrors them to perfection. There is no spur on the orchid's labellum, instead it has expanded into the shape of a bumblebee's abdomen, enticingly covered in the softest brown down bejewelled with a square spot of gold. Colonies of bee orchids flower for only short periods, so it is essential to drive drones into frustrated frenzies, seeking and suffering rejection, gathering and distributing pollen throughout the throng. Actually they do not have to behave like this, as if the orchids fail to entice any drones out on the town, their stamens, each with its two agglutinated masses of pollen, bend and fall into the hollow of the stigma.

Fly Orchis, *Ophrys insectifera*, are also blatant teasers, taunting the Digger Wasp's sex drive. The flowers are spread against three outer green sepals with a labium looking like a resting wasp with shining eyes, the petals forming brown wings, an anther like a probiscus and two sepals shaped like feelers. The allure is completed by the smell of a sexually mature female digger wasp called *Gorytes*. Digger wasps hibernate, the male emerging earlier than the female, and the Fly Orchis is synchronised to flower at the same time as the emerging male programmed to mate. Drawn by scent to the Fly Orchis he alights, the hairy labium guides him to take up the best position so that his sense of touch is stimulated. Certain of coition, he mates vigorously and the orchis responds by powdering him with pollen. Keen for further amorous adventures he moves on, depositing pollen on the stigma of the next orchis.

Fly orchis are difficult for humans to locate because they are only 10-30cm high with few flowers, of which only about 25 per cent mature after pollination. They grow in Europe from Norway to the Mediterranean region. Other species adopting similar tactics are: *Orchis speculum* by *Campsoscolia ciliata* a very hairy wasp species in Mediterranean countries, while *O.lutea* pleasures *Andrena*, a bee species who places its tail towards the centre of the flower while attempting to mate, so that the pollen clubs adhere to its abdomen. Unlike the bee orchid, the last three cannot do it themselves.

Why do **violets** shrink?

The Violet is known equally for colour and scent, a mix of red passion and blue cool which mirrors her attitude to approaching pollinators. We know spring has arrived when violets, primroses and daffodils start to flower, violets demurely appearing one at a time on delicate individual stems. However, theirs is an appearance mostly for show, while the rest of the garden is abuzz with assignations, couplings and fertilisation. The larger flowered broad-leaved violet, *Viola mirabilis,* disdainful of the efforts of others, lets her first maidenly flowers fade, but four months later, under her leafy canopy, a second discreet set of flower buds form. Within them are all that she needs to satisfy the urge to quietly procreate without the violation of the outside world, her stamens seek out her moist warm stigmas, embrace, fuse and fertilise. Her close relation the Sweet Violet, *Viola odorata,* occasionally toys with passing insects on first flowering but also revels in the high seed production levels of do-it-yourself and so shrinks away from the insect when it tries to alight. Appropriately the violet is in the cleistogamous group of flowers derived from the Greek *kleistos* – closed and *gamos* – wedding – so no 'My Big Fat Greek Wedding' here then!

What about the **scent** of violets?

The scent of violets seems elusive, one glorious waft then nothing, its Greek name of *ion* is recalled in its chemical composition ionine which dulls the sense of smell, making us unable to take a second positive scenting.

What can I **read** in **violets?**

In the language and symbolism of flowers, the colour and quietly determined growth of violets, have created the association of humility and the half hidden flowers the death of the young. On the other hand, the medieval floral language of erotic love was inspired by the resemblance the flowers share with female genitalia. Another relative the pansy, *Viola tricolour*, whose common name derives from the French *pensée*, thoughtful, is just that, hospitably providing a large lower petal that offers a well-designed platform for passing pollinating bees and bumblebees. If in doubt, have a look and see if you can see the yellow guiding spot, if you were a bee this also has a stronger scent than the other parts of the flower. The nectar is stored in a spur on this platform petal, its guard, which blocks the deep entrance, is described as 'a little man taking a footbath'; his 'feet', dangling just above the 'footbath' or nectary, secrete further supplies of nectar into the spur. We can only see the man's 'head' and 'neck', correctly the styles, which rub the bee's head as he pushes his probiscus into the nectar and kisses it with the stigma that forms the little man's mouth. The five fused anthers which form his coat, unbutton in three stages providing fresh pollen to sprinkle on the coats of visitors, increasing the chances of pollination whilst avoiding self-pollination.

Finally the Sorcerer's Violet is not a violet but a periwinkle – *Vinca* – which flowers like a large violet, but with deadly poisonous and evil associations.

Why don't **figs** flower?

Figs do flower but not in the usual sense, figs enjoy a symbiotic relationship with fig wasps, each species often having its own specific wasp. Look more closely at its base where the skin is tightly drawn around the ostiole which is actually a tiny orifice, it exudes its fragrance from this before it is ripe and while there is still some room for the wasps to manoeuvre inside. The flower lies within as tiny heads in the thready pulp, the gritty pips that form later are in fact the true fruits. Sensuous and fragrant, the soft pulp strains against its thin skin, whilst its interior is a network of soft whitish fibres set in purplish pink. Sounding more like a demolition specialist, this fig's call is answered by the fig wasp called *Blastophaga*.. Actually loss of wings is not unknown in the bid to squeeze in and then around the orgy of delights within. It is a chicken and egg cycle, so starting with the chicken: a young female wasp hatches in a fig and covered in pollen starts out on her life cycle, exiting from one ostiole and entering into another nearby.

A heavy schedule lies ahead as she pushes her ovipositor right down the fig's myriad delicate tubes; if she touches the bottom of the ovary she deposits an egg, if not she moves on. Her pollen is smeared everywhere and the tubes that were too long for her eggs ripen into seeds. Exhausted, her mission fulfilled, she dies. Four to twelve weeks later the wingless, sightless males emerge, although what they lack in sight is made up in mandible power. Fired by the most primitive of urges they devour the ovary walls to make contact with the females. Released from their ivory tower the females emerge covered in pollen, happy for dalliance before departing to restart the cycle. Despite producing all these attractions the figs in Britain are still waiting for *Blastophaga* to cross the channel, from the human perspective this part of their life cycle is surplus to our requirements. The fig wasp's work can be imitated with a small feather, by gently poking it through the ostiole and swivelling it around inside in a process called caprification.

However, in Indonesia's Gunang Pulang National Park the symbiotic cycle of the Strangler Figs, *Ficus caulocarpa, F. stupenda* and *F.sumatrana*, and the fig wasp, *Waterstoniella masii*, ensures a healthy distribution of figs for its exotic inhabitants. Animals such as wild pigs, civets and deer; birds like the Rhinoceros Hornbill and Red Crowned barbet, all feast on the fruit and even *Lexias* butterflies sip the juice.

What is a **plant** sport?

The following is a serious extract that reads like tabloid scandal. 'Chrysanthemums have a tendency to sport into various colours....Lord Alcester...originated as a sport from Golden Empress in the hands of an ex-policeman in Somersetshire, who was fortunate in fixing the sport and distributing it amongst horticulturists.' Advice from Edwin Molyneux in the third edition of *Chrysanthemums and their Culture* in 1888. In the horticultural world a 'sport' is a plant that has spontaneously changed from its parents. Chrysanthemums are prone to producing sports known as chimera, i.e. genetically distinct types which can co-exist, but successfully taking cuttings and 'fixing' these chimeral flowers is rare. A mutant ninja flower that does not play to the rules. Most mutations go unnoticed, either they wither because they are not passed on from the individual cell where they occur, or because the resulting changes are small. However, when a mutation occurs at a growing point, entire shoots may be affected, sometimes producing desirable characteristics such as variegated leaves, new colours or double flowers from which new cultivars can be derived. Darwin put it down to food, but it occurs naturally as a result of cosmic radiation, however, carefully orchestrated mutation can be achieved by applying an extract of colchicine taken from the autumn crocus, *Colchicum*, also known as Naked Ladies because their flowers appear separately from their leaves.

Where can you find **the most** excitingly shaped **flowers?**

Anywhere in the world, when the flower needs to attract specialist pollinators to its other attractions such as nourishing pollen and delicious nectar. Orchids take on many shapes and forms imitating bees, moths, a Lady's Slipper and flourish in almost every section of this book. The flower of the Bird of Paradise, *Strelitzia*, is so-called because its showy flowers so closely resemble the exotic bird. Beautiful as they are very few set seed in the wild, evolution seems to have made man with an artfully handled paintbrush a better pollinator. The flowers have a prominent blue spike which, if pressed, releases the pollen laden anthers. In the wild, the visiting sunbirds avoid this contact as it would mess up their clean feathers with moist, stringy pollen. They balance around the edge of the orange petals and drink the nectar unsoiled, leaving the *Strelitzia* unfertilised. However, at the dawn of its existence there would have been more reptiles such as lizards, which would have had to crawl across the flower to drink the nectar, thus triggering the blue spike and receiving a powdering of pollen. Flowers are not always what they seem, the dashing red flowers of the Poinsettia are in fact modified bracts.

Can **plants** pick up **pollen** from other **genera?**

Not without human interference. The sensitive moist stigma on a flower is super-receptive to its own brand of pollen but impenetrable to pollen of the wrong shape or those sending out alien biochemical signals.

What's the **difference between** a cross and **a hybrid?**

A cross is where two related plants i.e. two species in the same genera cross pollinate, usually when growing close together. A hybrid is not open pollinated but created by deliberately crossing two different varieties which may give the opportunity for dormant or recessive genes to come to the fore. The new plants often have hybrid vigour which means they grow and breed with renewed determination. Plant breeders can then select similar desirable plants from this diverse group of offspring, and self-cross them again and again until they attain the desired result. The desired result is that the variation in the offspring decreases, and so the plants all begin to behave the same. This hybrid seed is valuable for commercial growers who need to harvest the whole crop of, say, peas at the same time, but equally irritating for the domestic gardener trying to avoid a glut. Home saved seed from hybrid plants varies significantly and needs to be bought in each season. The next step is genetic engineering.

Why are so many night flowering plants white and scented?

White is a colour that remains conspicuous at night to the human eye, a tip worth remembering if you mostly sit in your garden in the evening. Both white and pale flowers are without ultra-violet reflecting surfaces, their luminosity and heavy, sweet scent carries great distances on the evening air which attracts pollinators such as moths and bats e.g. honeysuckle is pollinated by moths.

Where **can I find** the plant with the **hardest** seed?

Brazil where the nuts come from and it is seriously hard to crack them. The Brazil nut tree, *Bertholletia excelsa*, grows to 150m high, and it produces fist-sized pods containing up to twenty-five Brazil nut kernels. Fortunately it can live for up to 500 years, as both the flowers and kernels represent the plant equivalent of Fort Knox. The showy huge yellow

flowers secure their centres with a coiled hood, the males of the aptly named long-tongued orchid bee are alone in combining sufficient strength to open up the flower and have tongues that can reach the inner sanctum for pollen and nectar. After fertilisation, the pod develops such a hard shell that only the agouti and a squirrel have sharp enough teeth to strip off the husk; greedy for the nuts, they create stores for leaner times. Happily many are forgotten and seedling Brazil nut trees emerge.

This endemic cycle has been broken by a global demand for Brazil nuts. Around 450,000 tonnes are harvested annually in the Brazilian Amazon, and it doesn't take much imagination to realise the difficulties of a working grove. The more efficient harvesting from the wild by man, the less there is for agoutis and squirrels and correspondingly fewer self set seedling trees

The closely related *Leycis pisormis* in Trinidad, has a seed coating that can only be digested by bats whose efficient systems then disperse it ready fertilised.

Why does the **ivy leafed** toadflax turn **its face** to the **wall?**

So as not to drop its fertilised fruits. Look out on rocks and old walls for colonies of this herb whose Latin name is *Linaria cymbalaria*. It has small succulent trailing slender stems, the lower nodes providing anchor roots. Remarkably resistant to drought, the shiny leaves, tinged with purple, provide a cascading heraldic crest enamelled with pretty lilac flowers that adorn walls from late spring into autumn. Passing bees notice that the colours brighten as they approach the flowers: the lower lips are tinged with orange that close around the crimson-purple streaked spurred tubes or corolla, at whose stiffly haired carpet base lies the crimson ovary. A welcome mat for bees who head straight for the nectar and in the process set fertilisation in motion. The leaves of the ivy-leafed toadflax keep up outward appearances while the flower stalks turn their fertilised fruits gently towards the wall until they ripen and burst, so ensuring that the seeds are safely deposited in cracks and crevices in the wall.

Why should you 'plant **fennel** by your **kennel'?**

Its smell is said to deter fleas. It is also rampantly promiscuous with any other umbellifers, instead of the pure aromatic tastes of dill, parsley and chervil, fennel manages to inveigle its own signature flavouring into the mix.

Why are **crimson** flowered **broad beans** best in **splendid** isolation?

They must be produced by self pollination, so keep all their blushing blooms in close proximity so that they only fertilise each other. If you grow the white flowering varieties, they cross pollinate and the dominant whites send the recessive crimson genes into hiding. The good news is that seed production is usually high because most of the ovules are fertilised.

What **plants** are **aphrodisiacs?**

Simply ones that make you feel in glowing good health, so eat up your greens. A boost to your iron and vitamin intake increases your sense of well being and preparation for further pleasures. According to the Greek writer Strabo, Persian girls prepared for their wedding night by eating nothing except apples and camel marrow. The excitement of the exotic has included potatoes when they were first introduced. Potatoes are not the only tubers with expectations; the native orchid known as Long Purples, *Orchis mascula*, appropriately have two tubers as *orchis* translates as testicles: the plump new one is said to excite desire and was used for the historic spring tonic drink Salep; the slack tuber cooled desire but increased the chances of a female baby.

The small yellow and white flowers of jasmine were believed to represent the starry heavens. The tender white flowering Arabian Jasmine, *Jasminum sambac*, has the most heavenly scent. In Chinese, Batavian and Hindu cultures the flowerbuds were rolled into well oiled hair so that the exotic and erotic scent was slowly and increasingly exuded as the day passed into night.

The seventeenth-century herbalist, Nicolas Culpeper, recommended oil extracted from the hardy white flowering Jessamine, *Jasminum officinale*, 'a warm cordial plant governed by Jupiter in the sign of Cancer'. He lists a multiplicity of uses that would definitely increase well-being, such as warming the womb and removing diseases of the uterus, dispersing crude humours and opening, warming and softening nerves and tendons. The oil is still used today by aromatherapists for its soothing and relaxing effects.

On a gentler note, the white-flowered jasmine represents amiability and the yellow grace and elegance, pleasures to contemplate when sipping Jasmine scented tea. In the early twentieth century, Eleanour Sinclair Rohde perfectly encapsulated how jasmine wafts its charms:'The scent of jasmine has the richness of flowers such as hyacinths, the sweetness of the lily of the valley, and above all, an elusive quality which gives its perfume a fascination peculiarly its own'.

When do **plants** dance?

In the mitosis, commonly called the dance of the chromosomes. It is square dancing for plant cells in four movements: prophase, metaphase, anaphase and telophase. Firstly the nucleus divides into strands in a whirling gallop of kiss and chase; the rhythm slows as the dance enters its secondary movement, the heads engage in kissing while leaving their bodies sinuously to flail in freeform. Kissing fully accomplished, the flailing bodies gradually separate to face each other across the divide in the third movement. The fourth culminates in clustered regrouping like miniature hairpieces. The reel now completed, the resultant two neatly formed 'daughter' cells depart awaiting the next invitation to the dance.

Do plants have to be **happy** to be raised by **meristem** culture?

No, but the propagators are happy to know that they are guaranteed disease free material. The meristem is the very topmost tip of the plant, it is formed from undifferentiated tissue which has the capability of developing into organs or special tissues. This form of propagation is called micropropagation, an invaluable way of raising clean clones of rare, possibly diseased plants.

What is a **clone?**

A plant rooted from a cutting taken from the leaf, stem, branch or root which guarantees you will have a duplicate plant, running none of the risks of dominant and recessive genes that dictate the variations in seed raised plants. This is why they say you are you never alone with a clone.

What will I get if I **plant** my apple **pips**, peach **kernels** and **cherry** stones?

In the case of the apple pips probably a tree carrying indifferently flavoured apples. Occasionally there have been happy outcomes such as the Cox's Orange Pippin – apples with pippin in their name were originally grown from seed. Peach kernels are well worth sowing as they often come 'true to type' i.e. produce the same or a very similar peach to that you have just enjoyed. The famous fruit nurseryman Thomas Rivers, raised many new varieties from 1840-60 on his nursery at Sawbridgeworth in Hertfordshire, he also noticed that seed-raised plums were hardier. The parent plants of sweet and acid cherries are the Gean, *Prunus avium*, and the sour or Morello cherry, *P. cerasus*, both seed themselves freely and nowadays they are used as the rootstocks for larger sweeter fruits. Archaeological evidence shows that these cherries were eaten by people during the Bronze and Iron Ages. Thomas Rivers bred one of the sweetest cherries, Early Rivers. Earlier in his career in 1834, Rivers introduced the small sweet plum also called Early Rivers, which he had found among a batch of seedlings from a Plum Precoce de Tours which his grandfather had planted between 1770 and 1780.

Why **do you** need **more** than **one apple** tree?

Apple trees are self-sterile, the pollen grains on one tree's flowers cannot germinate its stigmas however attentive the pollinating insects are. It needs cross-fertilization which means you must select apples that blossom at the same time. This does not exclude crab apples: *Malus* 'Golden Hornet', sounding like another pollinating insect, is an excellent all round pollinator.

What makes
top fruit top?

Mating and dating for most top fruit trees such as apples, pears, plums and cherries takes the form of budding or grafting shoots of the finest fruits onto rootstocks that will dictate their height and ensure their successful growth. Rivers also acted as marriage broker for the first Californian orange growers who found that the Florida oranges did not acclimatise and thrive in their drier Mediterranean-type weather. In 1876 Rivers supplied orange trees raised from 'Excelsior' from his nursery in Sawbridgeworth, including a variety still grown called 'Valencia Late'.

The final fruit of his grafting labours was a pear which was named after his death at the 1888 International Fruit Conference. It is now the most widely grown and consumed pear variety in the UK – Conference.

5

Purposeful
Plants

What is the **most useful** plant in the **world?**

The palm tree of which there are about 2,800 species worldwide. In Venezuela they say 'The palm can live without the Indian but the Indian cannot live without the palm'. Alternatively there is a South Sea proverb: 'He who plants a coconut tree plants food and drink, vessels and clothing, a habitation for himself and a heritage for his children'. Without the hand of man the fruit has crossed oceans, kept buoyant by the thick, fibrous husk that surrounds its hard, leathery, watertight shell and hollow centre. It has settled on the sandy shores of every continent and island in tropical waters. The fleshy interiors provide the raw ingredients for oil, margarine and soap as well as being delicious as a tropical drink and as a culinary delight.

One of the hardiest is the carnauba palm which lives in the arid Andean regions of Ceará and Piauì whose prolonged droughts are broken by an occasional biblical deluge. Apart from an extensive root system the carnauba conserves waters by creating a thick wax coating over its leaves. The Cearense harvest the longest fronds and lay them out in the hot sun, the wax dries and peels off the desiccated leaves which are then beaten to extract the last of the wax. This can only be done on a small scale as only a certain number of leaves can be taken from these slow growing palms each year. Carnauba, or in Brazil *ouricuri*, wax can be used for furniture and floor polish, old fashioned carbon paper and a myriad decorative uses. The fronds are not wasted; they are woven into hats, hammocks and fishing nets. Young fronds are suitable for cattle fodder. If felled the trunks provide telegraph poles and bridge structures and the terminal bud can be cut for salad

Coconuts originally get their name from the Portuguese coco meaning grimace, although hopefully more of a smile now as holidaymakers sip their pina coladas.

When did **agriculture** start?

The earliest evidence is the Neolithic Revolution in the Near East and North Africa dating back to *c.* 9,000 BC. Here they grew wheat and barley as well as domesticating animals, by 7,000 BC they had added lentils and peas. In the Andes of South America they were growing potatoes and cucurbits around 8,000 BC, adding lima beans in 7,000 BC. If you have a taste for history, one of the 'Lost Crops of the Incas' Achocha, *Cylanthera pedata,* is still available, the good news is that it is tolerant of cool climates and shade, the bad that it is extremely vigorous. Its vines extend to over 4m (15ft) supporting cream coloured flowers that develop into 1.5cm (3in) fruits like gherkins. They are vitamin rich; if you don't eat them green the fruits mature to burst open revealing black edible seeds

By about 6,500 BC there was farming in Greece and around the Aegean Sea. Within a thousand years agriculture had spread up the Danube to present-day Hungary, reaching Germany and the Low Countries around 4,500 BC, crossing the sea to Britain around 4,000 BC. Meanwhile along the Mediterranean, agriculture had developed from about 5,000 BC. Possibly the best known early agricultural story is that of Ancient Mesopotamia and its rich alluvial plain between the Rivers Euphrates and Tigris – the aptly named Fertile Crescent. Originally skirted by the earliest farming villages dating back between 9,000 and 6,000 BC their numbers were swelled by colonisation movements during the sixth to fourth millennia BC. The swathe of land to the west and north stretching from the Mediterranean coast to the Zagros Mountains near the Persian Gulf was the natural habitat of wild cereals. These were harvested and improved by selecting ever fatter seedheads. The sophisticated Mespotamian practices included irrigation; unlike the gentle flood plains of the Nile, both the Tigris and Euphrates were subject to violent flooding just when the crops were growing. The agricultural need to establish dykes and canals to control the water also called for and resulted in structured political organisation.

What part did **chickpeas** play in the rise of **civilisation?**

The cultivation of chick peas can be traced amongst the founder crops that earned the Fertile Crescent its name. Zohar Kerem of the Hebrew University in Jerusalem has recently researched its nutritional benefits and has concluded that it can be cited as one reason for the rise of civilisation. He collected the rare wild chick pea, *Cicer reticulatum*, which dates back some 11,000 years, and compared its nutritional value with cultivated varieties. He discovered the amino acid tryptophan, the precursor of the neurotransmitter serotonin, in greater quantities in the wild variety. When increased amounts of tryptophan are taken in the diet this may improve performance when under stress and promote ovulation. The results therefore suggested that chick peas in the diet actively helped man develop physical and mentally in this acknowledged hub of western civilisation. So eat up your houmous.

What's the **difference** between **heirloom** and **heritage** vegetables?

Heirloom have been grown by the same family for generations while heritage have a traceable history. Both heirloom and heritage seeds are of great importance for the future viability of gene diversity. The International Plant Genetics Resources Institute has put fifty food plants on a high priority list, the most important being tomato, wheat, beans, cassava, sweet potato and coffee. In the last fifty years wheat varieties have been bred that yield twice as much. They have shorter stalks – not so good for thatchers, with a greater resistance to pests and fungal disease but, and there is always a but, the micronutrients have fallen, some say by 20 per cent or more. There is also the possibility that the changes in the gliadin protein in wheat could be associated with increases in allergy and intolerance.

When is **red** and **orange** better for you than **white?**

When choosing onions, sweet potatoes and sweet corn. The powerful antioxidant quercetin, which acts as an anti-cancer agent, is only present in yellow and red onions. On plantations in the American South, plantation owners prized whiter fleshed sweet potatoes while their slaves ate orange fleshed ones. White became a symbol of refinement; sadly this attitude still prevails in third world countries where orange fleshed sweet potatoes are one of the staples of food aid. In developed countries orange fleshed sweet potatoes are widely stocked and consumed for their excellent amounts of Vitamin A. The darker varieties of sweet corn are also richer in Vitamin A. Researchers are going back to the original wild perennial maize, *Zea diploperennis*, where they have traced disease and pest resistant genes that they plan to breed back into commercial varieties. In fact Mexican farmers still encourage wild maize to grow alongside cultivated maize to aid natural crossing which is beneficial to their crop – an active example of 'crop wild relatives'.

The wild maize, only about 1 inch long with tiny four-rowed ears of corn, was first domesticated around 5,000 BC in Meso America. Native Americans bred the parents of the modern varieties and Christopher Columbus brought back the first seeds in 1493. So apart from corn on the cob, how else do we consume maize? Corn starch to thicken, corn syrup in sweet drinks and snacks, and Bourbon is distilled from corn. We also eat beef fattened on corn; in Nebraska it is calculated at the rate of ten pounds of corn feed to one pound of beef and corn fed chicken at three pounds translating into one pound of flesh. We even brush our teeth with toothpaste containing sorbitol. Industrial uses include paper fibres bound by cornstarch, cornstarch in shotgun shells, fishing lures, toys, golf tees, nappies, ear swabs and cereal box liners, dustbin liners, and lastly we can drive away in ethanol fuelled cars produced using alcohol distilled from cornstarch.

How much
grass does a cow eat?

Cows need most grass when they are producing beef for us to eat, so to produce 20kg of beef protein, a cow needs one hectare of grass as opposed to the simpler equation above of ten pounds of corn making one pound of beef. It is worth remembering that one hectare of grass will include several varieties of grass as well as wild flowers and leaves that provide added protein.

Why is it good
to be in clover?

Emily Dickinson sums it up for bees:

'The pedigree of honey
Does not concern the bee;
A clover, any time, to him
Is aristocracy'.

It is good if you are a ruminant or a grower of green vegetables because clover is in the legume family and fixes nitrogen in the soil (see p. 18). Clover includes crops such as white clover, red clover, purple clover, yellow melilot, Lucerne, and the crimson fenugreek of Italy. There are twenty native species of *Trifolium* clover in the UK. So farmers with high milk yields and bumper crops are in clover in all senses. Like Hercules, farmers can rest after their labours and contemplate that the origin of the name clover is derived from clava, the club of Hercules.

Clovers are important bee flowers and their quest for the abundant nectar ensures good cross-pollination. The flowerhead consists of a standard petal shaped like a narrow draining spade, wing and keel petals. As the bee lands the keel petal steers the stamens and the pistil into dusting the chin of the bee with pollen. Off goes the bee and at the next port of call rubs his chin over the stigma. The robber baron insects also want to be in clover and take the easy route by perforating the flowers from outside and thrusting their probiscus through the hole to plunder the nectar.

How can **marigolds** help **growers?**

They are pretty to human eyes and distasteful to predatory pests such as nematodes, slugs and whitefly. The so-called French marigolds, *Tagetes patula*, produce a group of substances known as polythenyls that are toxic to nematodes. Organic farmers grow marigolds as part of a rotation, turning them into the soil after flowering as an ongoing deterrent; or, much the same but of shorter duration, as a green manure. They also use them as a dynamic duo, growing them alongside as cover crops; as well as farmers, gardeners can do the same to good ornamental effect. Traditionally the sunny flowers of the original marigold, *Calendula officinalis*, were believed to be a counterbane against poisons and the devil, symbolically flowering on each of the Virgin Mary's feast days, hence Mary's Gold.

What are **nematodes?**

Garden lowlifes, a type of eelworm that decimates crops of potatoes, tomatoes and other members of the solanum family. Their flexible bodies enable them to swim in an eel-like manner in thin water films between plant cells or soil particles. In the plant world many are predatory and are vectors for some virus diseases, others feed on bacteria or fungi. Cyst and Root knot eelworms both damage roots; stem and bulb eelworms, as their name implies, attack onions and bulbs; and then there are the self-explanatory leaf and bud eelworms.

What makes
blueberries so special?

They are full of vitamins and anti-oxidants, research has shown evidence of substances with cholesterol-reducing properties, they are said to be good for the bladder and for easing cystitis. Once you start eating them the claims multiply – slowing down ageing, improving your love life as well as improving your night vision and shortsightedness – an interesting global effect for the body. Blueberries thrive where the ground is poor and has a low pH 4.5–5.5, once settled they crop for fifty years. Ripeness equates with full flavour so at this point take off the rose tinted spectacles to ensure not the merest tinge of pink is left on the fruit or its stalk.

Why are oats
like horses?

The common oat, *Avena sativa*, and its main consumer, the horse, are both native to Tartary in Central Asia. About 2,000 BC when the domesticated horse was brought from Asia to Arabia and Egypt it brought the contents of its nosebag with it. The two travelled in tandem through the Ancient Greek and Roman Empires at which point oats acquired the classical name of *avena*. When it was discovered how well oats acclimatised to the cooler climates of Norway, Sweden, Ireland and Scotland they became and remain key cereal crops.

What happens
when **'horse'** is put
before **plant?**

It usually represents strength but not use, as in the conker-bearing Horse Chestnut, *Aesculus spp*, as opposed to the similar looking edible Sweet Chestnut, *Castanea spp*. Horsemint is a fairly tasteless thug in comparison with Peppermint, worse still is the acrid and bitter tasting Horsenettle, *Solanum corolinense*, also evocatively known as Apple of Sodom or Poisonous Potato. But hold your horses, what about the delicious condiment horseradish? Indeed it is strong but it is a powerful stimulant to the digestive system and a natural beneficial diuretic as it supplements the body's potassium rather than depleting it. It is a member of the Cruciferae family which also includes radishes, salad rocket and brassicas and so has the cancer preventative compound isothiocyanate – a higher bitter constituent. Collinsville in Illinois claims to be the horseradish capital of the world; it hosts the International Horseradish Festival each year over the first weekend in June. Competitive activities include the Horseradish root toss and horseradish golf using a club carved from a root. A round of 'chipping nearest the pin' can be followed by the Horseradish bagging contest to see who can get the most roots in a 100lb sack. Having worked up a hearty appetite you can enter with relish the Horseradish

Eating Competition – hot root spread on hot dogs. Field grown horseradish are cut into 2in lengths and planted in spring, fattening up over the summer season and are best dug after the frost has killed off the tops.

For the sake of your eyes, try to grind them while they are still fresh. Their flavour will alter according to climate and soil. Commercial varieties of horseradish are mostly known by numbers but American gardeners can choose between Bohemian, Swiss, Common, Maliner, Kren or, the biggest rooter Dusty Rhodes. It is traditionally used in Jewish cooking as a bitter Passover herb when the root and the green sprout are symbolically prepared together.

The roots of the Horseradish Tree, *Moringa oleifera,* which the Sinhalese call *murunga,* are used by them as an edible relish. It also has the name Oil of Ben Tree: ben from the Arabic word meaning an aromatic gum which is found in the bark while the seeds yield an oil, still used in perfumery and traditionally for lubricating watches and other delicate mechanisms.

Why not ride out with the herb that, according to Pliny, cured Chiron the Centaur of the wounds inflicted on him by Hercules – the Horse knobs or Horseknot or Horse snap more usually called Knapweed. It was traditionally used for love divining and as a tonic and a cure for sore (hoarse?) throats and catarrh.

When is a **bean** not **a bean?**

When it is a heritage seed called Mr Pound's Bean with bicoloured deep pink and pale pink flowers, a pod like a peapod and peas like beans. Peas are actually classed as beans and come in many forms – broad and runner beans, lentils, mung beans, chick peas and the ubiquitous baked beans. Menopausal women should be hot on their trail, all of the above contain phyto-oestrogens, meaning in simple terms plant rather than human oestrogens. A valuable source of green medicine as the plant oestrogens bind to women's oestrogen receptor sites so setting up a reaction that weakly mimics their own hormones.

How can you **read** a plant's **signature?**

Look at its colour, shape and where it is growing, from these outward signs ancient herbalists would read its inner characteristics and uses. Take Sphagnum moss which absorbs moisture from the atmosphere and the soil to create the perfect dressing for wounds, clean and ready moistened with the additional benefit of having antiseptic properties that help heal wounds. It looks like a coarse lint dressing that would have been applied to wounds. Damp places were notorious breeding grounds for lung complaints and several mosses have properties to strengthen the lungs as well as helping blood circulation. The traditional signature herb to heal tuberculosis would have been Iceland moss, *Cetraria islandica*, also found in other parts of Northern Europe. It is so mucilaginous that 30g (1oz) boiled in 550ml (1 pint) of milk or water could yield 180-210g (6-7 oz) of mucilage. With a spoonful of sugar and more boiling in milk it forms the base of a dessert jelly in Iceland.

The yarrow, *Achillea millefolium*, is a useful first aid plant if you fall when walking as it too staunches blood – its Latin name recalls that Achilles treated his wounded soldiers with the plant. As Shakespeare noted, the willow grows aslant the brook, as do the creamy white plumes of meadowsweet, *Filipendula ulmaria*, also found flowering sweetly in ditches. As both these plants grew in damp habitats, extracts were used for fevers and headaches in traditional medicine. In 1838 salicylic acid was isolated in meadowsweet and synthesised as aspirin.

What is a **lichen?**

It is what happens when a fungus and an alga take a lik'n to one another. It is described as a mini ecosystem looking like a plant but it is actually a compound organism of two or three parts. There are 3,600 species in North America alone. Their survival mechanism includes 600 chemicals unique to them which enable them to live in marginal environments and ward off attacks by bacteria, fungi and grazing herbivores.

Graphis elegans is a lichen that grows in raised dark lines on the smooth pale bark of holly leaving a pattern that looks like oriental script. The soil enriched *Peltigera aphthosa* forms a vibrant pattern on the forest floor carpets of British Columbia. This lichen hosts bright green algae and is peppered with dark warts holding nitrogen-fixing cyanobacteria. It nestles with starry mosses dependent on clean air, so any check in its growth acts an early warning device for pollution. The foothills of California's Sierra Nevada are a kaleidoscopic array of red, yellow, orange, grey and white lichens. The bright yellow lichen, *Pleopsidium oxytonum*, spreads lizard-like across the rocks, it is used medicinally and rejoices in the local name of Lizard's Semen.

The Salish people of the American North-West Interior recount the legend of how the tresses of the lichen, *Bryoria fremontii*, started when Coyote's long hair became entangled in a tree and was magically transformed into food hanging from branches in thick clumps. It is edible but one of the reindeer lichens, *Cladina stellaris*, is a real caribou treat. Caribou will nose through deep snow to reach and eat it. Safe to eat, these lichens are relished by Arctic peoples once they have been fermented in the caribou's stomachs.

People have harnessed these lichen substances – pigments, toxins and antibiotics – as sources of dyes and medicines. The lichen *Usnea* has served as traditional medicine worldwide and is now in several European antibiotic creams. Where would the Scottish Harris Tweed industry have been without the earthy smell imparted by lichen dyes which provide stalkers with a camouflage outfit that blends with the mottled patterns created by lichen-covered stone, heather and grasses. Equally the historical hue extracted from Mediterranean shrubby grey lichens soaked in stale urine that ensured ancient rulers were clad in royal purple.

How much
bamboo does a **panda** eat?

A great deal, pandas have evolved a very inefficient means of feeding, being dependent on bamboo which is low in nutritional value. They are condemned to browsing during most of their waking hours in order to stave off starvation. In China there are

four designated panda range areas in Sichuan and a further one in Shaanxi in Qin Ling. Fortunately, reaching heights of 12,359 feet, the Qin Ling forms a natural haven for pandas, it protects them from the Siberian blasts but is open to the south-east monsoons that bring rain and warmth. In this micro climate bamboo thrives plentifully. Actually panda mothers stop eating (and defecating) for twenty-five days after giving birth, baby pandas move onto bamboo solids when they are a month old.

Around the world there are about 1,000 species of bamboo of all heights and sizes, some have canes with diameters of over 30cm and the uses to which they are put are myriad. One manipulation is to grow the new young culms inside a square cube so the canes are a more convenient square cross-section.

What is **yellow** and the **world's** most costly **spice?**

It is the pistils of a crocus, *Crocus sativus*. 150,000 open flowers have to be harvested to yield 1kg of its bright red pistils which when dried are better known as saffron. The name Saffron is derived from the Arabic for yellow – *za'fân*.

How do **pigs** find **truffles?**

The world's finest black truffles, *Tuber melanosporum*, grow in the Périgord region of France searched out by the supersensitive snouts of blonde female pigs called *chercheuses*. Rather than grow, truffles appear near a host plant such as the truffle oak or *truffier*, and some species of both hazel and Austrian pine. They are reasonable guests providing their host trees with minerals from the surrounding soil by mycorrhizal association (see pp. 220-1) but, at the same time, their growth on the roots also stunts its development. The truffle is a fungus that grows in tufts of filaments, from 2in to 12in below ground and spreads by spores. Truffles exude a particular smell that top class trufflers can detect from 6m (20ft) even when they are 10in below the ground. The distinctive scent is also picked up by the damaging truffle fly, *Helomysa tuberivora*, who ruins the crops by laying its eggs in them. Dogs, badgers, foxes and ferrets have all been used to track truffles as well as close observation of the truffle fly. There is also a lesser 'cook's truffle', *Tuber aestivum*, which has a white centre and a faintly garlicky flavour.

Why do we need **toadstools** and **mushrooms?**

Fungi include some of the most important organisms in the

world and play important roles economically and ecologically. They are key to breaking down dead organic matter and so continue the cycle of nutrients through ecosystems. Among their many uses they provide drugs not least penicillin; the bubbles in bread and champagne; see also pp. 37-8 for drinks such as beer.

How can an Abyssinian kale speed up the supermarket checkout?

You won't find *Crambe abyssinica* on the vegetable displays because it is busy oiling the mechanism. It yields an oil rich in erucic acid that acts as a 'slip agent' to help open supermarket bags. It is also used in specialist heat proof inks on till receipts.

Why do peanuts bury their heads in the sand?

Peanuts flowered ornamentally in the gardens of Virginian plantation owners, but their slaves understood the nutritional value of the next discreet step. After pollination the flower stalk directs the immature fruit back into the soil where it matures in its pod some 8cm deep. Peruvians have been digging up these ground nuts since 2,000 BC. The Spaniards took plants back to Spain and Africa and then introduced them into Virginia. Their Latin name, *Arachis,* derives from the Greek *a* – without and *rachos* – branch and there are twenty-two species of both annual and biennial varieties. The wild *A. hypogaea* (below the ground) is no longer known in its wild state. The best commercial varieties are Virginia, Runner, Spanish and Valencia. Jimmy Carter's family wealth and that of other producers from farming peanuts is thanks to the pioneering work of George Washington Carver. Carver (1864–1934) recognised the commercial potential of growing peanuts and popularised it as an agricultural crop

Dr Rudolf Diesel originally designed his engine to run on peanut oil.

How many **barrels** of pure **petrol** can you harvest from **a** **hectare** of Euphorbia **tirucalli?**

The dangerous white sap of the leafless Petrol Plant contains large amounts of hydrocarbons, enough to yield 125 barrels of pure petrol per hectare. Should you find yourself dehydrated in the Canary Islands the ascending sap from the interior of the *Euphorbia canariensis* provides a refreshing drink. Make sure it is not descending sap as that is virulently acrid like most Euphorbias.

How do **dock leaves** help nettle **stings?**

This is one of the best known plant cures. It works immediately as there is the psychological relief of finding a dock leaf after you have been stuck by a nettle. Then rubbing the affected area helps disperse the irritant. The sting lies in the downy hairs each of which have a sting in a sharp, polished spine which is hollow and arises from a swollen base. This base is formed of small cells which contain bicarbonate of ammonia, the venomous, acrid fluid that makes them sting. The good news is that nettle stings help clear toxins from the body. They were offered to the Romans after bathing as a cure for rheumatic joints, by urtication or flogging with nettles. This continued to be a traditional remedy for chronic rheumatism and the loss of muscular power. Its beneficial uses against rheumatism are currently the subject of research by Dr Colin Randall of the Peninsula Medical School in Plymouth. Should you be going bald combing with nettle juice daily reputedly stimulates new hair growth.

Nettles are one of the few plants not nibbled by rabbits as the stings attack their sensitive noses; however, a patch of nettles is a haven and body builder for the caterpillars of small tortoiseshell and Red Admiral butterflies.

When did **humans**
cotton on to **cotton?**

Cotton, *Gossypium herbaceum*, has origins in both south Asia and Central and South America and has a history that dates back to before 800 BC. The earliest account appears in the Hindu mythology of creation which refers to the cultivation, spinning and weaving of cotton in ancient India. There are records that it was introduced by Sennacherib to the Upper Tigris at Khorsabad in 700 BC. On his triumphal return from India in 326 BC Alexander the Great brought back cotton. About the same time the Greeks were growing cotton as a garden ornamental and the Egyptians in Upper Egypt as an agricultural crop. Cotton in the Far East followed the same introductory route as Buddhism and garden design, starting out in India reaching China and Korea by 600 AD, then in 789 a Chinese junk laden with cotton seed was driven off course and shipwrecked on the Japanese coast where they also started to grow it. The Moorish invasions of Europe introduced cotton as well as saffron and rice.

In Central America the ancestors of the Aztecs, Mayas, Columbians and Incas were cultivating cotton, spinning cotton thread and weaving intricate cotton cloth. The sophisticated weaving methods resulted in fabrics that ranged from muslin to velvet, sometimes they wove in animal fur and birds feathers. They also went into battle in armoured coats made out of cotton.

Vast cotton plantations were worked by slaves through the eighteenth and nineteenth centuries in Brazil, the West Indies and United States. Today the 'cotton belt' in the United States stretches from Florida across to Texas – the largest production area in the world.

What is **cotton** fibre?

It is the epidermal hairs from the seeds of *Gosspyium*. The fibres consist of hollow cylindrical tubes, narrowing at the end, that are 15-22μm in diameter. The fibre walls consist of 90-96 per cent cellulose mixed with about 5 per cent water and small amounts of pectins. The tubes flatten when dried and naturally curl or twist like a ribbon.

What put the **blue** in **jeans?**

'King of the Dyestuffs' indigo originally came from *Indigofera*, a dyestuff plant used by the ancient Egyptians, Greeks and Romans. Later it crossed the Atlantic to the Caribbean and into America. The first successful grower was Eliza Lucas who managed the family plantations in Charleston, she reaped her first successful harvest in 1741. Her husband helped to improve their techniques by interviewing French prisoners brought to

Charleston from the Caribbean. This American indigo was unrivalled in quality. In 1850 Levi Strauss 'invented' blue jeans, now dyed with a synthetic indigo.

Where does kapok come from?

The fluff that surrounds the seeds of the *Ceiba pentandra* commonly known as the kapok tree. This lustrous yellow floss is resistant to decay and water so has been put to many purposes. Kapok is used to stuff bedding, upholstery and life preservers and it acts as an efficient insulation against both sound and heat. It has clusters of white flowers all of which open together late at night and into the early hours of the morning. There are about fifteen species of *Ceiba* including the *C. aesculifolia*, the pochote kapak whose green seeds are much enjoyed by parrots and parakeets.

Can plant fibres replace fibreglass?

Yes, resins are being reinforced with plant fibres to create rigid structures called biocomposites. These are being used for car components such as non woven plant-fibre mats and for external body panels that are proving to be as strong as aluminium.

Why do vegetables
avoid travelling into
the wild
and **unknown?**

Quite simply they would disappear, unable to fend off lesser suitors who would reduce or negate their esculent or tasty edible characteristics.

Where do
tomatoes come from?

Tomatoes originated in the high altitude regions of Chile and Peru and their spread around the world is thanks to man. Juicy delicious tomatoes first attracted animals by their scent and sweet taste which ensured the spread of wild tomato seeds via the animals' digestive systems. The Spanish Conquistadores noted small, yellow tomatoes in Mexico soon after Columbus sailed the ocean in 1492. The Spanish introduced the seeds to the Philippines, the Caribbean, Italy and, of course, Spain. Globally they have undergone spontaneous variations as a result of mutation and cross pollination which is why they taste and look so different when grown in England or South-East Asia. Yellow is actually the dominant colour, red tomatoes get their colour from the pigment lycopene.

Why do **figs** fast forward your **digestive** system?

Whether you eat fresh or dried figs they are a gentle laxative. The chief constituent of the fresh fruit is dextrose of which they comprise about 50 per cent; they also contain flavonoids, vitamins A and C, acids and enzymes. The laxative properties are related in the fresh fruit to its saccharine juices and in the dried to the seeds and skin. Properties that were bottled and marketed as Syrup of Figs.

The Biblical fig, *Ficus carica*, is indigenous to Asia Minor, Persia and Syria but was introduced across the Mediterranean region and later to Britain, firstly by the Romans, and again by Thomas à Becket. Fig trees were often planted by the outside dining room or *triclinium* of the Romans, offering fruit, shade and their leaves as readily available lavatory paper. There are many different cultivars with skins ranging from deep purple to an almost translucent green, the flesh can be the brightest pink or hazy purple. In *Colour Schemes for Flower Gardens* Gertrude Jekyll dedicated one chapter to 'A Beautiful Fruit Garden' in which she describes the fig in almost elegiac terms:

> To pass the hand among the leaves of the Fig-tree, noting that they are a little harsh upon the upper surface and yet soft beneath; to be aware of their faint, dusky scent; to see the cracking of the coat of the fruit and the yellowing of the neck where it joins the branch – the two indications of ripeness – sometimes made clearer by the drop of honeyed moisture at the eye; then the handling of the fruit itself, which must needs be gentle because the tender coat is so readily bruised and torn; at the same time observing the slight greyish bloom and the colouring – low-tone transitions of purple and green; and finally to have the enjoyment of the luscious pulp, with the knowledge

that it is one of the most wholesome and sustaining of fruit foods.

The fig does not confine its benevolence to being a laxative: the wolf that suckled Romulus and Remus is said to have rested under a fig tree; Adam and Eve used the leaves to cover their naked shame and in the Old Testament book of Isaiah, Hezekiah used the fruits as a remedy for boils. In more recent medical history it has been employed in the treatment of catarrhal nose and throat complaints. The milky juice of the stems and leaves is acrid, which on the one hand can help remove warts and on the other raise blisters.

Which **mulberry** can you make **paper** from?

The inner bark of *Broussonetia papyrifera* from China and Japan was used by the Chinese to make paper, hence its common name Paper Mulberry. Although related to the mulberry the leaves are too rough and coarse for the fine palate of the silkworm and the fruits are only enjoyed by poultry.

Can I eat snowdrops and daffodils?

No, they are poisonous but they contain galantamine which is widely used to treat Alzheimer's disease. The daffodil variety Carlton has notably high levels of galantamine and is now being grown commercially in order to extract this valuable medicinal principle.

How can Christmas Trees cure bird flu?

The rare shikimic acid that is used to make the drug oseltamivir (Tamiflu) that is used in the treatment of bird flu is found in star anise. Research has shown that it can also be extracted from the needles of most conifers and most usefully discarded Christmas Trees. Although readily available every January, at the moment the cost of extraction and storage outweighs its development.

Why does
eating rhubarb make my teeth
feel furry?

Rhubarb stems contain large amounts of oxalic acid in oxalate crystals. This is released when cooking breaks down the cell wall structure.

What is
the **fungi** that puts **alcohol** in our
glasses?

It is a single celled fungus called *Saccharomyces cerevisiae* which can turn sugar-rich squashed fruit and mashed up grains into an intoxicating substance. Its second name, *cerevisiae*, was coined to describe the early beers brewed from barley and whose name echoed Ceres the goddess of cereals.

6

Naming and Shaming

How should I
address a plant?

Never be afraid of the more formal Latin binomial nomenclature, you can travel the world and still be talking about the same plant. After closely and methodically studying the sexual characteristics and habits of plants Carl Linnaeus established plant classification by flowers, particularly stamen numbers, and fruit. Linnaeus created a big sex scandal in eighteenth century Europe when he published his *Species Plantaram* in 1753 followed by *Genera Plantaram* in 1754; conversations about his explicit survey of plant breeding were banned in polite circles.

He divided the Plant Kingdom into Classes, Orders, Families, Genus, Species and Variety – an epithet to which a cultivar or breeder name is sometimes added. So in reverse order every species belongs alone or with others to a genus, each genus to a family, each family to an order, orders into classes and finally four divisions (see p. 77). Binomial nomenclature uses two of the classification categories: the plant's genus – its generic name, and the plants species – specific name.

Common names make you feel on more familiar terms, speaking in the local dialect. Starting with binomial nomenclature take *Parietaria officinalis*; the humble Pellitory of the Wall which is one of the nettle family, Urticaceae. Members of the nettle family are distinguished by the explosive mechanism with which they scatter their pollen. *Parietaria* is the generic name, it is derived from the Latin *parietarius* meaning 'of walls' matched with the specific or descriptive name of *officinalis* which indicates plants that were formerly of commercial value and sold as medicinal plants in shops. Its officinal or medicinal properties were prized by no less than the playwright Ben Jonson, 'A good old woman . . . did cure me With sodden ale and pellitorie i' the wall'. It is rich in nitre and has a diuretic and cooling effect. Herbalists used it in the treatment of diseases of and stones in the bladder and kidney as well as dropsy and stricture.

Common names around Europe echo its habitat and its uses: in France its ability to root into walls *perce-muraille*; in Germany, the Netherlands and Italy its high nitre content *Glaskraut*, *Glaskruid* and *Erba de Vetri* respectively. Another species is the *P. ramiflora* meaning flowers shaped like oars because the insignificant flowers have bracts shaped like oars.

The Pellitory flowers are bisexual and the stigmas are unusual on two counts: firstly, some are red and some are white; secondly, they protrude before the calyx opens to reveal the full flower, shrivelling and falling off before the stamens open and release their pollen. The stamens are incurved within the bud, and as the bud expands they spring out scattering a cloud of pollen.

What are **native** plants?

Native plants include all indigenous varieties which will have evolved in tandem with their local ecosystem and so tend to be neighbourly and friendly. Naturalised plants are species that have established themselves having been introduced by man. In England some such as woad are a delight, others like Japanese knotweed a dangerous thug.

How **fast** is a **landrace?**

It is completely stationary because these are varieties of plants that have developed *in situ* which have enabled them to evolve to their surroundings. They have adapted to the local climate, to the characteristics of the underlying rock known as lithology and to the characteristics of the soil known as pedology. Names rather than rosettes identify the local winners: peas such as Lancashire Lad, Glory of Devon and Kent Blue.

What is an **outbreeder?**

These are plants that cross with another variety, a nuisance if you are trying to save seeds of plants like carrots which happily cross with other umbellifers such as cow parsley and wild carrot. A blessing if the new plant proves to be an improvement.

Who was **Dioscorides?**

A Greek physician in the Roman Army, a pharmacist and botanist. As he travelled around the Roman Empire from 50 to 70 AD, he noted which plants the local tribes used. His writings are invaluable because he was the first to realise the importance of how local climate and soil conditions affected plant growth, he studied and recorded all parts of the plant from root to seed. He recorded names in Latin and the local languages of Egypt, Africa, Persia and Armenia as well as their uses. 600 plants were profiled in his treatise *De materia medica* along with animals and minerals that were of medicinal use. The Yam family, Dioscoreaceae, are named after him and specifically the group of edible yams, *Dioscorea*.

Little did Linnaeus know when he honoured Dioscorides that these subsistence yams contained active ingredients that revolutionised twentieth century living – the contraceptive pill and cortisone which was until then only available in the pituitary gland of bulls. The active ingredient is Diosgenin which is the precursor to progesterone and both it and cortisone can now be extracted in commercial quantities. There are some 600 species of yam which climb from tuberous roots – a staple (and sometimes poisonous) source of starch in tropical and subtropical regions; they include the Chinese Yam, Air Potato, Hottentot Bread and Cush-Cush. Alternative names give a clue to their ornamental strengths as they twine and brighten pergolas and trellises – the Chinese Yam with its white cinnamon-scented flowers sounds prettier with its alternative sobriquet Cinnamon Vine. The male flowers of the Air Potato, *Dioscorea bulbifera*, form 10cm (4in) spikes, while the female flowers are a more showy 25cm (10in).

Why should a **Dutchman's** Pipe carry a **health** warning for **gnats?**

Not just gnats, but its pollinators in general. Known botanically as *Aristolochia spp.*, one of the biggest *A. grandiflora* is also known as the Pelican Flower. With a delicate fishy odour, its red flowers are patterned like leopard skins with brown spots bordered by yellow. Inside, the corolla tube has stiff hairs that act like an eel trap, holding the pollinator until the mission is completed when the hairs wither and freedom beckons. The hardy climbing Dutchman's Pipe, *A. durior*, is also known as birthwort, a use reflected in its Latin name taken from the Greek – *aristos*, best and *lochia*, childbirth. You might easily mistake the flowers *A. salvadorensis* as the face of Darth Vader. *A. arborea* looks like a mushroom in order to attract the flies that pollinate it while the *T. tricordata* has long petals like fly papers for the same purpose.

Why is **Aristolochia** useful for **snake** charmers?

Aristolochia serpentaria known as snakeroot was chewed by Native Americans and applied to snake bites. One drop from *A. clematitus* lulls snakes for snake charmers who also anoint their bodies to provide immunity to attack.

Can you **find Jack** in the **Pulpit** in any **church?**

No, but you might find him in the churchyard preaching against the host of names he is also known by which expose his sexual, devilish and deadly properties which include Bobbin and Joan, Cuckoo Cock, Angels and Devils, Devil's Men and Women, Adder's Food and Frog's Meat. Geoffrey Grigson in *The Englishman's Flora* lists no less than ninety-one common country names for the plant correctly addressed as *Arum maculatum.*

The inflorescence takes the form of a prominent phallic shaped spadix that is purple tinged, sheathed in an encircling pale green spathe. The polite names of 'Lords and Ladies', or the seemingly bucolic 'Cuckoo-pint', (despite the fact that pintle is the old name for penis) both refer to its overt suggestion of copulation. The spathe becomes warm to the touch just before opening to expose the spadix and releases a warm waft of urine.

When cooked, the root was served as Portland Sago, because the crop was harvested commercially from the Isle of Portland. It was said to be both strengthening and venereal. Small quantities of the cooked plant are reputedly a sexual stimulant. However, all parts of the fresh plant, from its tuber to its leaves and bright red berries are poisonous. A few berries on the tongue can make it swell to the point where swallowing is nearly impossible. If children eat the berries they will die agonisingly within ten to twenty hours. The raw root yields a milky juice that has an initially insipid taste followed rapidly with a burning and pricking sensation. The vice of lust and its potential murderous qualities have excited names such as Adder's Meat, Poison Fingers and Soldiers and Sailors. Last but not least, possibly the longest country name, Kitty-come-down-the-lane-jump-up-and-kiss-me.

What about **Jack** in the **Pulpit's** private life?

It is decidedly lurid. The flower is constructed like a trap, the smell of urine on the tip of its spadix is to lure moth flies, *Psychoda phalaenoides*. Below the spadix three sets of florets are hidden, accessible by the narrowest circular opening, however,

as the walls of the spathe are well oiled they are like a helter-skelter for the alighting midges. The oiled walls, with downward pointing warts, ensure no saving foothold, but a precipitous slide down past a wreath of the first sterile florets that are fashioned with hairs that block the exit. The ride speeds up as the insect tumbles past the male florets into another garland of barren flowers before landing on a cluster of female flowers. Each female floret has one ovary and one stigma. At this point the captive visitor hopefully obliges by pollinating with its pollen load. Strengthened with sap flavoured with sugar from the stigma the insect will soon regain freedom. The stigmas wither within the day simultaneously opening their anthers to shower the visitor with pollen. The barriers are removed – the hairs wither and the oily spathe skin wrinkles providing a rough surface for the midge to scale. Off the ride the midge cannot wait to try it again and heads off from the Lords and Ladies to sample the Soldiers and Sailors. Individual arums attract numbers that would satisfy any theme park with up to 4,000 midges in a single plant.

How can **Lady's Mantle** help women stay **young?**

By alchemy; the Lady's Mantle, *Alchemilla mollis*, gets its Latin name from the old alchemist's belief that the droplets that form in its furry leaves had alchemical properties – possibly to turn base metal to gold. Belief in the power of these droplets extended to them offering the elixir of youth. Ladies who wish to sample the elixir should venture naked into the garden at midnight and drink the droplets to secure eternal youth (and possibly pneumonia).

What **part** of the **Chaste Tree** made people **chaste?**

The seeds were known as 'monk's pepper' as they were taken to lower the libido. The common name derives from the *Vitex agnus-castus* – *castus* – spotless or chaste – and it is an aromatic deciduous flowering shrub. Today its fruits are used to make a pungent, bitter-sweet herbal medicine for menstrual and menopausal complaints and involuntary ejaculation.

What puts the **Devil** in plants?

Traditional and country names to warn you that the plant has poisonous and potentially evil constituents. Sometimes the Devil goes under the name of Satan or Old Man. Devil's Berries, Devil's Cherries, Satan's Cherries and Devil's Rhubarb are all alternative names for *Atropa belladonna* more usually called Deadly Nightshade. *Atropa* named for Atropos, one of the three Fates whose task was to cut the thread of life. It contains the poisonous principles of atropine and hyoscyamine (also found in henbane). You would be well advised to avoid Bad Man's Oatmeal in Northumberland; far from being a warming breakfast dish it is also known as Devil's Blossom and Devil's Flower, and most commonly known as Hemlock, the deadly poison chosen by Socrates.

What do
Strangler Figs strangle?

Other trees in the rainforest. At some point in their evolution they realised that there was not enough light on the forest floor. Fortunately however their fruits are greedily consumed by birds who then dropped the digested seeds from a great height. The hot, humid conditions of the tropical rainforest encourage the accumulation of decayed leaves and mosses in the clefts of branches – this is the target the Strangler Fig seeds hoped for and so hundreds of species were able to migrate up into the forest canopy. The germinating seeds put initial roots into the rich mulch, then the young leaves form so that photosynthesis can start. The leaves are very waxy to prevent transpiration as the cleft of the branch can only hold limited water and the seedlings are exposed to tropical sun Once established and having escaped predation by insects, their clinging roots spread out from the cleft and embrace the host tree in what, over the ensuing decades, becomes a stranglehold.

Birds are not the only creatures to help spread the seeds: in addition, gibbons and long-tailed macaques swing by for some fruit salad. Their droppings pebbledash branches and bark exposing the seeds for *Polyrhachis* ants who take them back to their tree-crotch nest site. The seeds that they do not eat are left to become potential new Strangler Figs and so the forest canopy colonisation is continued.

Do **dandelions** make you **wet** the **bed?**

Yes, beware of eating dandelion leaves after midday as they are a diuretic, but valuable if you suffer from water retention. Most diuretics deplete the body's potassium but dandelions have the added bonus of being rich in potassium. *Pissenlit* is the French translation for dandelion, *Taraxacum officinale*, and the Old English name was Piss-a-bed. Dandelion root has the skill to re-educate the liver to reduce its sluggish tendencies and behave with vim and vigour.

Its juice has been used to remove warts and in Dorset dandelion wine was said to be good for kidney troubles and indigestion.

Can you blow your **nose** on a **handkerchief** tree?

No, the handkerchiefs are actually large white bracts that cover an ornamental tree from China, the *Davidia involucrata*. It was first discovered in 1869 by a French Jesuit missionary, Pére David, whose name it celebrates, in Boaxing (Mupin) in China. Such were its ornamental properties that in 1899 the young Ernest, later to be nicknamed 'Chinese', Wilson was despatched to bring back seed. Dr Augustine Henry kindly met him and gave him a sketch map of where he had also seen a specimen some 1,000 miles away from David's original sighting. Henry's map encompassed some 20,000 sq miles. Wilson travelled 1,000 miles up the Yangtze river, up the rapids above Ichang to Badong and then on foot following the tracks of salt smugglers. Then, unbelievably, he found the exact house where Dr Henry had stayed. Dr Henry was well remembered and the villagers led Wilson to the spot where Henry had described the *Davidia* in full handkerchief. That night Wilson wrote in his journal 'one more little cup of bitterness to drain' – the tree had been felled and made into a wooden house. He retraced his steps but did not return empty-handed, he collected a few of the loveliest shrubs that adorn gardens – *Azalea indica, Deutzia scabra, Jasminum floridum, Vitex negundo* and perennials like *Anemone hupehensis* var *japonica*. Wilson decided to venture south west from Ichang into David's original territory and, joy of joys, there was a 50ft *Davidia* in full flower. He 'drank in the beauties of this extraordinary tree' which 'stirred by the slightest breeze . . . resemble huge butterflies or small doves hovering'.

What is
vegetable **ivory?**

The hard white nuts of various tropical trees which provide a more cost conscious alternative. The two most commonly used are from the doum palm, *Hyphanae thebaica*, and the tauga, *Phytelephas macrocarpa*. The former is included in one the earliest Egyptian wall paintings of a garden dating back to 1,600 BC. The nuts of both these trees have a brown fibrous rind with a homogeneous white or yellowish white meat. The good news for artists is that the nuts are much softer than ivory so easier to carve – look more closely at buttons and beads.

When is **a rose** not a **rose?**

When it is a Rhododendron: its Latin name uses Greek words to describe it – *rhodo*, rose and *dendron*, tree. When it is a primrose, prim, a contraction of the Latin *primus,* referring to being the first or spring flower like a delicate rose. Primroses and primulas have given their name *primuliflorus* to describe pale greenish flowers.

Can you **buy** shares in **Brompton** Stock?

No, but the land on which they were bred would be an excellent investment and its names offer a richly scented trail. The Brompton Park Nurseries extended over 100 acres on the land that now lies underneath the Natural History, Science and Victoria & Albert Museums in London. In 1681 four distinguished gardeners, Joseph Lucre working for Catherine of Braganza, Moses Cook for the Earl of Essex, John Field for the Earl of Bedford and George London for Henry Compton, Bishop of London, decided that action needed to be taken regarding the lack of standardisation in the naming and introduction of plants. They took out the lease on Brompton Park, Kensington and founded the nursery. After 1687 it was run by London and Henry Wise.

By 1693/4 they were employing twenty men and two women and carrying a stock of 40,000 plants. London and Wise 'aimed to suit with Versailles' so they bred the erect bushy biennial Brompton Stocks for spring bedding and to fill low box hedged parterres sweetly and elegantly. There are several types of Stocks in the *Matthiola* species, noted for their fragrance and named for the Italian physicist and botanist, Pierandrea Matthioli (1500–77).

Do **vampire** orchids **suck** blood?

No but they look as though they might. They are in a genus suitably named *Dracula* that have trailing petals that look like fangs with many equally cleverly named types. *D. chimaera* originates in the mountain jungles of Colombia, Ecuador, and Peru. The white lip of *D. bella* quivers in her fragrant flowers of pale yellow spotted with brownish crimson. The seriously hirsute *D. tarantula* is outlined in purple to the very tips of the 'fang' tails within which the yellowish sepals are decorated with purple dashes.

When are
flowers candid?

When they have shiny white flowers as in the Madonna Lily, *Lilium candidum*, symbol of purity with stamens as the Venerable Bede wrote 'for a soul sparkling with divine light'. Those that are *candidissimus, -a, -um* are very white, *candicans* are shining or woolly white, sounding more dog-like is *canescens* which describes plants with off-white or ashy-grey coloured hairs.

How many **animals** in
the plant **menagerie?**

Almost as many as on the planet and many are contained within this book: horses, bees, flies, butterflies and moths have been described, linked with orchids, hogs and beans. What about planting a *Lilium formosanum* whose fragrance attracts the Virgin Tiger Moth, *Apantesis virgo*, into the evening garden. The plant zoo ranges from Wolfsbane, *Aconitum*, used to poison meat left out for wolves to the soft pupescent leaves of *Stachys* known as Rabbit's or Lamb's Ears. The ear of a mouse, the snout of a pig, the eye of an ox sound like a brew to be used by witch, toad and snapdragon flowers. The down of pussy willow, the uselessness of Goat's Rue, *Galega*, and the scattering of Hen and Chicks, *Chenopodium*. It is really a case of looks can tell.

What is a **bonobo** power **bar?**

The herb *Haumania liebfrechtsiana*: it is unusually rich in protein with very little indigestible fibre and devoured by bonobos or pygmy chimps in the Democratic Republic of Congo.

What are **tannins?**

They are the first line in defence used by trees against predators, the highest concentrations of these noxious chemicals can be found in bark, seed coats and protective tissues.

What has **'wings** that were meant to **fly** across **continents**; ... a standard which is **friendly** to all nations; and ... a **sweet** prophecy of **welcome** everywhere'?

The answer is a sweet pea, according to the Revd. W. T. Hutchins writing in 1900 of the Bi-Centenary Sweet Pea Exhibition held at the Crystal Palace, in terms that resonate with religious evangelism. Sweet peas are in the *Lathyrus* family. The name was coined by the Greek naturalist Theophrastrus (*c.* 370–286 BC) who was the first to write a systematic classification

of all known plants in *An Enquiry into Plants*. *La* means 'very' and *thoures* 'stimulating', because unlike garden peas, *Pisum*, the seeds have an irritant effect on the stomach. The exact origin of the sweet pea is unknown, it may have been Sri Lanka, however, in 1699 Father Cupani sent the first seeds from Sicily to Robert Uvedale. Uvedale was the headmaster of Enfield Grammar School who had received criticism for lavishing greater attention on his plants than his pupils.

The tri-centenary of their introduction was marked by the seedsmen Unwins with two new cultivars: Robert Uvedale which has rich carmine flowers with white bases to wavy petals; and a free flowering maroon sweet pea called Oliver Cromwell. And why? As a young boy Uvedale, in an act of Royalist defiance, stole a tapestry which covered Cromwell's coffin. If you are looking for really sweet sweet peas the grandifloras in lavenders, blues, mauve and the deeper colours are heady. If you want sunny but not so sweet peas choose oranges and salmon.

Where did the **Tree of Heaven**, Ailanthus altissima, **come from?**

The Moluccan Islands, where it was named Ailanto; it grows so quickly it was thought to touch heaven. It was introduced into Britain in 1751 from North China and is extremely tolerant of pollution. Sometimes it is kept cut right back in order to encourage the juvenile growth which has striking ash-like pinnate leaves that can be up to 1m long. The flowers are inconspicuous and the male trees have less than heavenly-scented blossoms but this is outweighed by the attractive clusters of orange- and red-winged fruits that form in August and September on the pollinated female trees. Trees allowed to grow to full size specimens branch out in a form that is reminiscent of a gigantic stag's horn.

Where in the **garden** can you find **smoke** without **fire?**

Where the *Cotinus coggyria*, better known as the Smoke Tree, is growing. Tiny purplish flowers mass at the end of the branches creating pink to purplish plumy panicles that look like smoke. It is also called Wig Tree, Jupiter's Beard and Purple Fringe Tree. Behind the ornamental smoke lies a history of utility: in Greece and Russia the plant was used for tanning and dying leather, wool, and silk.

Will **Ilex vomitoria,** the Yaupon **Holly,** make me **sick?**

Yes, the dark green-blue leaves of this holly were harvested by Native Americans in South Carolina to prepare a strong brew that was used during ceremonial rituals at the opening of their councils to cause regurgitation. It contains more caffeine than any other North American plant and was used by early settlers to make a lighter tisane, hence it's other common names of Southern Tea Plant and South Sea Tea. In Florida and Louisiana it was traditionally used as the best remedy available for yellow fever.

Could I make **candles** from the **Candleberry** tree?

Yes, by boiling the grey berries of *Myrica cerifera* which are both covered with a white waxy coating and contain an oily substance. The candles will be dark green. Up until the mid-nineteenth century they were made in the United States: Peter Kalm, the eighteenth century Swedish botanist, observed that the candles burned better than tallow and when extinguished gave forth a pleasant aroma. Also known as Southern Wax Myrtle, Bay Berry and Candleberry Myrtle, the berries were also a source for wax for soap making.

7

Peculiar Pests and Beneficial Beasts

What **plants** are **spongers** at the **feast?**

Mistletoe is one of the best known parasites. However, it does make a small contribution to its own survival through having leaves, as well as providing oaks and apples with seasonal decorations. Plants which have neither their own leaves nor roots plunder what their neighbours can offer. Even their names sound like social leeches – Dodder, Broomrape, Balanophorales and Rafflesia. Dodder, *Cuscuta europea*, germinates in the soil but without any food reserve, the embryo literally feeds upon itself. A slender first root anchors into the ground, giving support for the young thread-like red stem to rise up looking for support. Not just support, favourite targets are hops and, as the stems make contact, they produce suckers which contain conducting tissue intended to suck the goodness from the host plant to the Dodder. No plant needs the hard work of roots when they have food on tap, so once surplus to requirement, they just drop away. Another variety *C. monogyna* found in France has acquired a taste for vines, others use flax, thyme, clover and gorse. Clovers are also prey to Broomrapes, *Orobanche*, which fasten to their roots as well as selected trees and shrubs, they are notable for having no chlorophyll, sending up dingy flowers from their host root. Balanophorales are the tropical equivalent of Broomrapes, and include the biggest flower in the world, *Rafflesia arnoldii*, profiled in Chapter Three (see pp. 94-5).

A host of unpleasant parasites are represented by fungi, such as mildews, rusts, smuts and blights, unloved by farmers and gardeners alike. *Cordyceps* is a species of fungi that are parasitical on insects, spiders and even truffles. They could play leading roles in horror movies. One such is *Cordyceps sphecocephala*, a West Indian variety which attacks a species of wasp, *Polistes*; attaching itself to the head, the wasp continues to fly around until it is outweighed and killed. The New Zealand Vegetable Caterpillar, *C. robertsii*, sows itself behind the head of the caterpillar, *Hepialus virescens*, growing up 20cm (8in) in length. Others sow themselves in the bodies of larvae and pupae buried in the soil or among leaves. Lastly two with more gourmet palates: the Snake's Tongue fungus, *C. ophioglossoides ophio* – snake, *glosso* – tongue, which feeds in pine woods on the Hart Truffle, *Elaphamyces variegates*, and its close relation the Clubbed Cordyceps, *C.capitata*, which also freeload from another Hart Truffle, *E. granulatus*. However, its presence is of use to man: the latter truffle is subterranean and difficult to find except when infected by these eerie clubbed spore masses which show priapically above the soil leading human truffle hunters to their prize. A parasite of willow *Lathyraea* is related to toothwort. Ergot is a parasitic fungus that attacks a wide range of grasses in wet seasons, most seriously rye, (see p. 3)

What feeds **pollinators?**

The liquid high-energy sugary nectar and the protein in oil rich pollen. Insects also take supplies back to their larvae which in turn make tasty snacks for birds, mammals and pond life. Flowering early, Rosemary offers a late winter/early spring sip of nectar whilst the pollen and nectar on ivy at the close of the year attracts Comma butterflies and helps bees and queen wasps stock up on protein before winter. The nectar in some plants like blueberries is not easy to get at and ignored by honey bees with more on offer; however, wild solitary bees are prepared to make the effort. When planting blueberry bushes it is worth creating a small high rise in crumbling bricks or soft stones for one such bee, the mason bee.

Which **creature** is the best **pollinator?**

The *Hymenoptera* family which includes over 100,000 species of membrane winged insects such as bees, bumble-bees, wasps, gall wasps, digger wasps, ichneumon flies, ants and saw flies. Heading this field are bees of which there are 2,000 species, busy in action and sound, making far more floral visits, in a bid to gather enough nectar and pollen to feed themselves and their young.

How do **insects** measure **intelligence?**

In the insect families, the longer the tongue the greater the intelligence. No plant wants to entertain insects who just plunder the pollen and nectar, so they have shaped themselves against idle pilferers. The nectar from white and yellow flowers is generally easily available in trees like the Elder, however, the white blossoms of fruiting Cherry partially conceals its nectar in a tube designed for the longer tongued bees, butterflies and moths. The ornamental yellow flowers of the Laburnum are specially shaped with carefully placed, concealed pollen and nectar, accessible only to bees. The irregular flowers are held by a bell-like calyx, its upper part is divided into a two-toothed lip at the back, fronted by a three-toothed lip. Although the flowers are horizontal, like the iris it has a 'standard' or upright showy petal. The nectar is at its base contained in a cushion-like swelling on the outer face of the tube formed by the stamens. This is the landing strip and arrival lounge for the pollinating insects. There are ten stamens in all, five alternate ones have larger anthers than their fellows. The filaments of all ten stamens are joined to form a tube surrounding the one-chambered ovary, which contains a double line of several ovules down the one side of its wall. The long style is bent and raises the stigma above and beyond the anthers. Stamens and pistil lie within the keel.

Mediterranean herbs such as thyme, hyssop and marjoram tend to be nectar-rich and draw the happy buzz of bees and gentle wing beat of butterflies. There are no indigenous bees in New Zealand or the Faeroe Islands, so flies have taken on their pollinating role.

Why is the **Indian rhino** a beneficial **beast?**

He is regular and clean in his daily habits. After a day gently grazing his favourite grasses and the hard potato-like fruits of the Trewia tree he heads for a wallow in the river. Relaxed he emerges and defecates on the mud banks of the river. This benefits plant, tree and rhino: the seeds of the grasses that have avoided fatal grinding in his molars emerge ready to germinate and provide future feeding en route for the river. The fruit of the Trewia tree is too hard for monkeys or birds, so is dependent on being sown in so propitious a spot – open location, good light and manure – by the digestive system of the rhino.

Which are the **best British** insect pest **predators?**

Hoverfly larvae, followed by ladybirds and their larvae share top billing. Hoverflies suffer from their resemblance to wasps, they are smaller and hover rather than fly like spitfires, do not sting and are entirely beneficial. In fact their diet consists entirely of pollen and nectar. Ladybirds are unmistakeable with their red enamelled armour with black spots that opens to allow flying. Hoverflies are attracted by yellow umbels such as tansy, dill and fennel, the yellow flowers of lilies and hypericums, but, best of all, are the flowers of morning glory and the poached egg plant.

Both are champion destroyers of aphids, but hoverflies are the most efficient. Although the parents eschew aphids, their larvae like to gorge on them. So they lay their chalky white eggs among colonies of aphids, thus ensuring a food supply when they hatch two or three days later into slug like larvae with tapering heads. They are green or cream in colour growing up to 12mm long. During their larval stage of two to three weeks, they annihilate aphids with the added morsels of caterpillars and thrips. After one to two weeks' pupation, adults first emerge in May. Up to three generations can be produced in a year. They overwinter in the soil or leaf material as pupa.

Ladybirds munch a wider range of aphid species with a predilection for cabbage aphids, *Brevicoryne brassicae*. Again the offspring are more important than the parent. Ladybirds lay their yellow luminescent eggs, which look like tiny grains of rice, in clusters on stalks and leaves. The 5-10mm long larvae are blue black with orange spots, with a jaw development looking like two sickles. In a lifespan of just two to three weeks, they make the Hungry Caterpillar look like he was on a fast; with considerable dedication, they gorge about 300 aphids each day – with quick arithmetic this accounts for over 6,000! Pupation lasts from about a week to ten days, when the adults emerge to restart a process that can produce up to six generations in a season. Sadly their survival rates are lower than hoverflies, as they are less adept at sourcing good aphid supplies and are at the mercy of predation and cannibalism.

How do **aphids** damage **plants?**

They operate worldwide, especially on agricultural and horticultural crops: aphids on cabbages, melons, peaches, plums, apricots, potatoes and in cottonfields, colonise and then chew up the leaves of their living hosts. Reduced leaves means less photosynthesis, resulting in weakened growth and a poor harvest. Not only that but they can be harbingers of plague and pestilence – either by contamination or transmission of plant pathogens such as viruses. Take the cotton aphid, A. gosspyii, it is also a vector to more than fifty viruses and does not confine itself to cotton; any juicy cucurbits – pumpkins, cucumbers, gourds – are welcome. However, they need to watch out for the parasitic wasps that will bring them under control.

How do **pea aphids** carry mosaic **virus?**

Their feeding stylets serve as hypodermic needles which they do not clean between use, so they pick up virus particles from one host and then inject them into another. Having successfully over wintered, the pea aphid moves from alfalfa to peas early in the season, colourfully transporting and transmitting mosaic viruses. Naturally they graze on available plants, as they voyage from summer to winter quarters and *vice versa*. Any specific viruses they pick up remain viable on the mouth parts or within the bodies of the species that are vectors. The symptoms of mosaic viruses are light and dark discolouration and/or colour breaks on the leaves, stunted and malformed leaves and sterility of the flowers.

Mosaic virus is not confined to peas: tobacco mosaic virus (TMV) is capable of infecting species from more than 150 genera including tomatoes and peppers; while cucumber mosaic virus (CMV) can infect 750 species including spinach and petunias.

Where do **aphids** hide?

Trees, hedges and the soil provide winter and summer hosts for resident pests. The cotton aphid favours wintering in Catalpa or Rose of Sharon, before a summer of crop devastation. The Rosy apple aphid over winters as eggs on apples, moves to narrow leaf plantain for the summer, then back to apple at the end of the season. The Soybean aphid over winters as eggs laid near buds on common buckthorn, moving to soybeans for the summer, then back to buckthorn. The aptly named Carrot-Willow aphid winters in willow and, apart from summering around carrots, is not averse to damaging parsley, dill and coriander.

Which **Great Plains** beetle has **become** a serious **menace?**

The Colorado potato beetle. In its first incarnation, when buffaloes roamed the Great Plains, it survived on the indigenous buffalo bur. A member of the poisonous nightshade family, the beetle mastered digesting the toxins without self-harming. The native prairie plants could not sustain settlers so they planted the more wholesome potato, also in the nightshade family, which provided enjoyable fast food for the Colorado potato beetle. Pioneer travel introduced the voracious beetle across North America, a rapid breeder and adaptor, it has outrun every insecticide designed to decimate it and maintains its pestilential status. A potato called 'NewLeaf' has been genetically engineered to produce its own insecticide, one nibble on any green part spells death to the Colorado potato beetle. However, despite the big fast food outlets wanting the perfect chip, they have bowed to public pressure and are not ordering it. So 'NewLeaf's days seem numbered.

When is a **wasp** useful?

When it is a parasitic wasp like *Diaeretiella rapae* that works inconspicuously, not least in British domestic gardens. They help control the caterpillars of the large and cabbage white butterflies, as well as those of the diamondback moths. The adult wasps are black or brown, ranging in size up to 10mm long. There are different species of wasp tailored to their chosen prey e.g. aphids or caterpillars. The adults feed on nectar to help develop their eggs, which they then deposit directly inside their prey, many of whom are our garden pests. The eggs hatch in a few days. The larvae remain inside for a few weeks feeding on the guts of the prey, forming a pupa from which the adult will emerge after four to five days. The effect on aphids is to mummify them and the adult parasitic wasp just cuts out an exit and emerges. In general wasps only take nectar for themselves and carry insects back for their young in the nest.

Wasps are not, however, as efficient at pollination as bees, because they only take enough nectar for their personal needs and they seek out flowers with easily accessible nectar glands. However, there are flowers that are specially adapted for pollination by wasps such as the tuberous figwort, *Scrophularia nodosa*, snowberry, *Symphoricarpus rivularis*, and broad leaved helleborine and violet helleborine. The alluring smell of Catnip that sends sane felines into ecstasy, has much the same effect on parasitic wasps, its scent approximates to that of breeding aphids. Disappointing for the wasps, but good news for the gardener trying to lure in this aphid predator.

Which **plants** offer no **hospitality** or **rewards** for pollinators?

Charles Darwin was fascinated by the myriad different and curious ways that the pollinating mechanisms of orchids had evolved, (see p. 87). The following four could be sued under the Trade Descriptions Act, for attracting pollinating insects by gross deception, offering them neither pollen nor nectar as reward. The orchids of South America offer three, supplemented by one from Australia. The *Oncidium* species with large yellow and brown spotted flowers tremble in the slightest breeze. Several species in Ecuador look like an invading bee, thus provoking the local bee population into wasting precious energy warning them off, in the process having pollen lumps fastened onto their heads, which they take to the next head-on attack. There is some justice: the *Oncidium* is a popular orchid with florists so the flowers often end up in a vase.

The *Coryanthes* can be found in Central and South America, the huge flowers hang over like an oversized cockscomb. Inside the labellum is vaulted over with fleshy ridges and two side entrances. It contains a reservoir and overflow pipe which is fed with copious amounts of fluid, secreted by two glands shaped like horns. Charles Darwin noted: 'The most ingenious man if he had not witnessed what takes place, would never have imagined what purpose all these parts serve'. The overflow pipe keeps the fluid exactly level, and also forms a furrow beneath the anthers and stigma. The gigantic flowers are a draw for bees, who do not fly in for the nectar but instead to gnaw off the fleshy ridges. Jostling to get a taste, some fall back and the scent is so intoxicating that they drop into the reservoir. And the only way out with heavy wet wings? By way of the furrow which conveniently knocks the stigma, leaving pollen clubs fastened to the bee's back. If in his drunken stupor he dips in the same flower again, it will not self pollinate as the anthers become receptive later.

Gongora gives the *Euglossa* bee a theme park water ride when he turns his tail downwards as he arrives to alight on the labium. The intoxicating scent and fluid from the labium send him into a spin and he slides down the petal on his back gathering pollen as he rides.

The flower of the *Drakea* of Australia looks like a small excrescence and smells like a female wasp, but holds the necessary allure to draw in an innocent male wasp. No sooner has he landed, than the labium swings rapidly forward and brings the wasp's head in contact with the anther. The pollen strikes and retains its club shape, but bends forward to form a pollen club fringe perfectly aligned to hit the stigma of the next *Drakea* as he continues his waspish ways.

How do **carnivorous** plants get **hold** of their **insects?**

In five devious traps: the pitfall, the passive fly-paper, the active fly-paper, the snap-trap and the bladder. The first pitfall category includes the Pitcher plants which look and operate like their name. They have slightly open lids which shield the mouth, prevent evaporation and dilution by rain. Around the rim are inward pointing teeth called the peristome which is like a fence preventing the prey from escaping, but aiding entry are convenient ladder-like ridges up the outside of the pitcher.

The passive fly-paper trap includes the *Byblis gigantea* in Australia which is a small 45cm bush. It has long narrow leaves covered with stationary stalked glands which are stud-like in shape; their flattened ends produce a droplet of a viscid fluid. The prey sticks on alighting, as it struggles smaller glands nearer the leaf exude more sticky fluid. The fluid gradually builds up until it actually dissolves the prey.

You may not think this is particularly passive, however the active fly-paper trap includes the *Drosera* which has almost entire leaves covered in insect trapping glands. They can also move their glands to capture struggling prey and reposition them for comfortable digestion. For an insect it is like landing into drying concrete.

The snap-trap takes the form of a major stem with whorls at intervals of five to nine leaves. With the exception of flowering

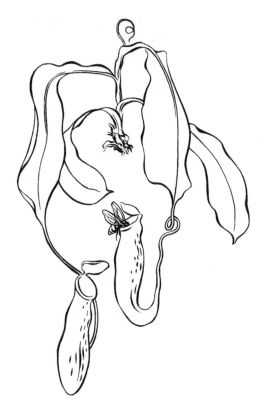

whorls, each leaf terminates in a two lobed trap. The hapless prey brushes trigger hairs as it enters and the two lobes close rapidly. During the ensuing bid for freedom the other edges close leaving the prey imprisoned in a chamber until it is digested. The final category concerns the bladderworts: Fairy Aprons is the common name for several bladderworts, such as the *Utricularia*; the name relating to the bib and skirt of their pretty flowers. These are plants of wet flooded areas and the danger lies in their network of submerged leaves. On these leaves are small 'bladders' with an inward-opening door with trip hairs at the entrance. First they expel air, so from outside their convex side walls become concave. The sophisticated door is sealed against the water pressure on the outside. Tadpoles and other small fish innocently swimming past trigger the trip hairs, causing the bladder doors to open and suck them in. The doors clang shut, opening only to add to the store.

Why do small **ermine** moth **caterpillars** spin silken **tents** across bird **cherry** trees?

So that they can feed on the leaves safe from the predations of birds and parasitic ichneumon flies. Strictly speaking, the web is actually produced by the communal larvae of the small ermine moth and the silken tent also shields them from temperature extremes during cold nights, after having consumed what would have been the shelter of the leaves. They also enjoy undisturbed feasts on hawthorn and blackthorn bushes which are both in the Rosaceae family.

Which **mulberry** leaves can make **silk?**

The White, *Morus alba*, introduced into Europe via the 7,000 km Silk Road. Silkworms have been farmed for at least 5,000 years in China to chew through the leaves and spin their valuable thread. James I was keen to establish an English silk industry, so introduced a thousand mulberries for national distribution and even planted the present day site of Buckingham Palace as a mulberry garden, unfortunately they were *Morus nigra* – great fruits, useless leaves. During the Dig for Victory Campaign in WWII young women were encouraged to keep silkworms so that they could weave their own wedding dresses!

White and Black mulberries were grown in Mesopotamia and Ancient Egypt, then across the Roman Empire. Mulberries do not mind being all alone with their leaves palely loitering as the trees are self fertilising. The inconspicuous catkins carry uni-sexual flowers. Rather than each flower forming a fruit they cluster together to create the raspberry-like fruit which are at their best when they ripen from dark red to black.

What **nourishment** does **Kidney Vetch** offer?

The Kidney Vetch is the sole source of food for the caterpillar of the Small Blue butterfly in Great Britain.

Why do **birds** clamour to **drink** at the **Passionflower's** bar?

The nectar is intoxicating and plentiful. Passionflowers collect large amounts of nectar in a cup shaped hollow that is on public display. The birds can be as raucous as they like, as the private domain of her ovary is beyond reach, however, the action in the bar above gently fuses the stamen and style below. Not only birds but humans have been entranced by the passionflower. The plant hunter, Ure Skinner, wrote back from Paraiso to James Veitch of the beauty of a red passionflower and 'another passionflower, very pretty and sending forth a scent such as can be equalled to a thousand violets. I have sent home a box'. He died of yellow fever shortly afterwards.

How do **bats** make **sausages** grow on trees in **Ethiopia?**

They are the pollinators of the *Kigelia Africana* commonly known as the sausage tree because of the shape of its fruits. In Ghana the Ashanti name Nufatene means hanging breasts and they are a symbol of fertility. In Kenya the seeds are believed to enhance male sexual prowess. The fruits provide edible treats for elephants and baboons; fortify home-brew beers, and local healers in Malawi and Zimbabwe make skin salves from the bark.

How far can bats **stick out** their **tongues?**

In 2006 scientists awarded the prize for the longest tongue extension to the tube-lipped nectar bat, *Anoura fistulata,* whose tongue is one and a half times its body length. It stores the 9cm tongue under its rib cage when not sipping nectar from the bell shaped flower *Centropogon nigricans.* This is the equivalent of a cat lapping milk from a saucer 60cm away. The bat and flower have evolved into their unique relationship in the cloud forests of the Andes.

Some bats live exclusively off pollen and nectar and so need a great deal of it. These bats can be relied on to do a thorough job because they are warm blooded, or more correctly homeothermic, and therefore, need great quantities of nourishment to maintain their body warmth. The flowers of the balsa tree, *Ochroma pyramidale*, cater for this, providing 1.5 cubic cm of nectar. On the pollen front, the baobab tree, *Adansonia digitata*, provides the pollinating bats with 1,500 to 2,000 stamens in each flower. The bat's forelegs are formed into wings held stretched out by four fingers. The thumb is in the middle of the front edge of the wing and has a powerful claw which is used for landing or climbing. The back feet are

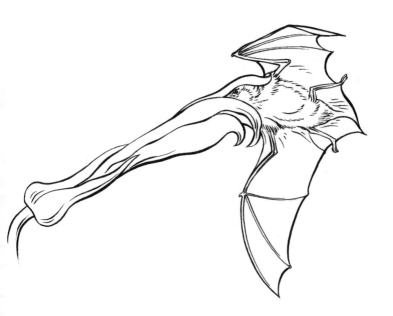

free and also have powerful claws. Some bats hover for nearly a second in front of the flower and suck the nectar with their tongues which have hairs on the last quarter. One species has a tongue of 76mm and a body of 80mm long.

Bats pollinate many larger nocturnal flowers, being rather heavier than insects and moths the flowers are proportionately sized. Most bats alight, using the claws on their thumbs grip the flowers and stick their heads inside. The claws leave marks, making it possible to determine when a bat has pollinated a flower. Anthers and stamens are near the flower opening, a good tongue-length from the nectar, or they extend outside the flower. These flowers are strong enough to bear the bat's weight and tolerate the shock of the landing, often the openings are wide enough to allow the bat to enter and so pollen fastens onto its fur. Bats have also adapted: the flower-pollinating species have much smaller ears making entry into the flowers easier: those that live off insects have well-developed ears, and find them by sending out sounds and then listening for the echo.

Bats have special scent glands which play a part in reproduction, and flowers aim to replicate that sensual attractant. The scent differs from bat species to species but is usually described as sour, musty, cabbage-like or sickly. The bats nocturnal habits are catered for by the anthers being open and the flowers being scented only at night, when they open only once, before withering. Most bat-pollinated flowers hang away from the plant on very strong long stalks as it would be difficult for a bat to manoeuvre between leaves and twigs.

What other **plants** are bat **pollinated?**

Trees like the banana, *Musa*, and the kapok, *Ceiba pentandra* or, in its native setting, the house or tender bedding plant Cathedral Bells or Cup-and-Saucer vine, *Cobaea scandens*. The liana, *Mucuna gigantea*, has huge flowers hanging on rope thick stalks that grow to a height of 20m while the flowers hang down to 1.5m above the ground. The flowers of at least a thousand tropical tree species grow on tree trunks with no leaves or twigs and many are pollinated by bats; in some the fruit is thought to be eaten by bats, and so it also has to be accessible. Bats are the pollinators and seed dispersers of several cactus species, feeding on their nectar and fruit – the Saguaro cactus for example, or *Carnegia gigantea* in Mexico. They also pollinate about sixty species of agaves, including the source for tequila and the Mexican Agave, now growing wild in Mediterranean countries, which has a huge inflorescence of yellowish flowers that point upwards and stand clear of the leaves. Bat pollination occurs mainly in the tropics of Africa, Asia, Australia and the Americas. Their territory also extends as far north as Arizona and up to 3,400m above sea level in the Andes. The jade vine, *Strongylodon*, a tropical creeper with flowers that look like polished jade stones is another example, it opens at night to be pollinated by bats.

What other **animals** fly by for a **little light** pollination?

Arboreal mammals such as Australian marsupials, Indonesian squirrels and flying foxes.

What gets **pollinated** underground?

A species of Australian ground orchid, *Rhizantella*, which is pollinated by termites. The orchid dips its head under the soil to make it more convenient for the termites to set about their work of pollination.

Where do you find **fish** in **trees?**

In the flooded Várzea and Igapó Forests of Amazonia. Many of the trees in these forests depend on fish eating their fruits during times of flooding, with their digestive systems then dispersing the seeds. In coffee growing regions of the monsoon area of South-east Asia the important rains of March to May are called blossom or mango showers.

Why do so many **plants** like ants in their **pants?**

Plants and ants have co-evolved to their mutual benefit over millions of years, to such an extent that there is a group of ant-plants. Apart from the shelter of hollow stems and pockets of accumulated soil on branches, plants have evolved leaves with hollow cavities to provide shelter for ants. Plants such as anthuriums provide food with edible seed coatings. After supping, the ants plant the seeds, which is one of the ways plants manage to establish up in the forest canopy. The ants return the hospitality by being efficient housekeepers and sentinels as well as nutrient providers and pollinators.

Indigestion is not just a human problem. Dinner for the Pitcher Plant, *Nepenthes bicalcarata*, is taken from tasty drowned insects in its liquid trap. A balanced diet is essential but if the decomposing reservoir of insects piles up the juices turn foul. However, the help of strong swimming ants is at hand. Enter the *Colobopsis* ants conveniently and comfortably housed in its tendrils; in a communal effort, they scavenge the larger insects like crickets, hauling them up the slippery walls of the pitcher. Thus settling the Pitcher Plants' digestive problems.

The orange-red spores of a fern in Borneo provide an oily feast for the *Philidris* ant, the ants return the favour by dragging debris down to the fern roots thus adding nutrient-rich compost to the infertile sandstone. This incidentally also helps another plant, *Dischidia,* which contributes to the system by housing ant nurseries in its slender white roots which are not in the ground but within its leaves, the waste from the nursery ensures food for its roots.

How do **ants** help **trees** in **mangrove** swamps?

The *Myrmecoda spp*, is an epiphyte that is not rooted in the soil but around the trunks of the trees which grow in Australian mangrove swamps. *Myremecoda* can only live with the help of ant-lodgers who inhabit the prickly football-sized swelling that forms most of the stem. Ants are excellent housekeepers using the holes on the surface for exits and entries into their various chambers. In my lady's chamber, the queen steadily produces eggs with nearby nurseries for raising young larvae, all with smooth light-coloured walls. The ants also create a lavatory block where they deposit their droppings and food remains, rich in phosphates and nitrates. These chambers have darker walls with uneven warty growths from which the *Myremecoda* absorbs the precious nutrients needed for its growth and flowering. The flowers are used by the Apollo jewel butterfly to lay its eggs.

Why does **Black Eyed** Susan secrete **nectar** on her calyx?

To attract an ant bodyguard who, while enjoying this nectar, wards off the predatory wasp, *Xylocopa*, from thieving her nectar without having the decency to undertake pollination. The protective presence of the ants forces the wasps to enter through the proper opening – they still get their nectar but provide pollination through the proper channels. There are several plants around the world noted for their dark eyes but this one is *Thunbergia alata*.

Who takes an **Acacia** by its **Mexican** bullhorn?

Ants for whom the cup shaped leaves and large hollow thorns of the Mexican bullhorn provide a des res. The ants also keep up the surrounding grounds by grubbing out seedlings at the base and overhanging branches from other potential arboreal competitors. The thorns on a bull's horn acacia, *Acacia sphaerocephala*, are joined together at the base hence the common name; they are about 5cms long. Not only are the sharp thorns a deterrent but the inhabitant ants protect their host from predators. First to arrive is the queen ant who gnaws a hole at the base of the young thorns just big enough to gain entry. Ready mated, she then lays her eggs. The worker ants that emerge are vigilant in their destruction and consumption of any nibbling insects that might damage the acacia's leaves. This is an empire that expands and will go to war with any other ant colonies taking up residence – the battle is bloody, severing limbs and casting out wounded enemies. Apart from insects, the ants enjoy a variable feast in-house provided by the acacia. Throughout the year they sup from nectar that flows from glands along the lower part of the leaf stalks. On the tips of its leaflets the acacia produces small orange beads that are rich in fat; worker ants harvest and prepare the beads for the larvae. The beads are cut up into fragments that it packs into a special pocket on the underside of the larva, just below its head. Rather like a built-in nose bag the larva bends its head and sticks its jaw into the ready-made meal. A perfectly balanced partnership.

What **use** is a **bumble** bee?

Apart from being better tempered than honey bees, they are much more industrious and there are more than a score of bumble bee species in Europe. Although they are just as social as honeybees, they live in smaller communities (could this account for their better temper?). They are of great importance as pollinators because they are strong and very hairy with long proboscis and acute senses. The longest probiscus on British bumblebees belongs to the pleasingly named *Bombus hortorum* coming in at about 1.5cm (½ in). Despite appearances of bumbling around indiscrimately fumbling up flowers' skirts, they learn quickly and have an excellent memory with regular habits that flowers have adapted to. Despite their quiet diligence all except the queen die at the end of the season; the fertilised queens tuck up for winter underground in moss, grass tussocks, stone walls and bark crevices. Mild winters are playing havoc with this as some worker bumble bees are also surviving.

What **colours** do bees **see?**

Bees see in ultra-violet which shifts their colour perceptions in the following way: our violet transforms into shades of blue and purple; where we see blue they perceive lime green, green is yellow and yellow is red.

Is the **primrose** pale and **interesting?**

Of course, what would spring in the countryside be without buttermilk primroses gently drifting through woods and along shady banks. The five petals of each flower are delicately held by its clasped calyx as though it were a nosegay. Subtle differences lie at her very core – just two, but offering an interesting diversion for the essential business of pollination. You need to look into her yolk yellow centre to spot the difference: one has a long styled stigma that reaches up to the centre of the calyx but keeps the powdered stamens within a tiny club, hence the name of pin-eyed flower; the second has a short styled stigma which stretches out the stamens like an open cluster within its thrum-eyed centre. Apparently not a male/female bid for pollination but a different but equal offering, both Primroses offer a honeysweet fragrance and hospitality day and night. Bumblebees, drones and butterflies are welcome to dip their

assorted proboscises to varying depths within her nectary. Moths make nocturnal visits to sample the fresh dew that forms on her flowers. Traditionally to take the Primrose Path symbolised the choice of an easy life of lust and idleness.

Where can you find crabs, tadpoles and snails tanking up on tropical cocktails?

In the rich reservoirs of the Tank Bromeliads which can have a capacity of up to 10 litres (2 gallons) and thrive in high humidity with good sunlight. Not only do they catch rain, but falling leaves and unwise insects which combine to make a rich brew. Euphonia birds use the tanks for their nests, droppings from the chicks provide the plant with nutrients. Diligent tree frogs lay their frogspawn to hatch under moist forest leaves, the tadpoles develop and crawl onto their parents backs to hitch a lift up into the canopy to find individual tanks for further development. Crabs provide housekeeping skills, they clean up, collecting snail shells which remove calcium before laying their eggs. Parent crabs then feed insects including malarial mosquito grubs and snails from this larder to their hatched young. Males hit the road while females stay close to mother. Last but not least the carnivorous bladderworts also feed on the water and passing primates and snakes on its contents.

How can **snails** help to **keep** the **aspidistra** flying?

The aspidistra has the reputation of an urban survivor echoed in its other common names – Cast-Iron Plant and Bar-Room Plant. A hardy pot plant that would thrive or at least survive in poorly lit city parlours. It is noted for its leaves but, like other more ornamental plants, it looks forward to the joy of pollination. Far from overt, flowering takes place at the base of the plant and the flowers are a dull purple, but they serve their purpose as pollination is carried out by snails or slugs.

What is the **hottest** of **thermogenic** plants?

The dead horse arum, yes it smells like a dead horse and has a warm male part. This wafts its enticing aroma to tempt pollinating beetles. The male pollen-producing stamens mature a day earlier than the female stigma, providing beetles with a steamy nightclub in which they mate while whiling away the time.

Does **coral** suffer from **tooth** decay?

Healthy coral lives symbiotically with single-celled algae until threatened by pollution. Pollution leads to an invasion of bullying macro algae which release sugars. These sugars diffuse into the coral, fertilise the bacteria and increase harmful microbial activity. Oh that coral could brush it away.

What did **dinosaurs** eat?

Inspection of coprolite or dinosaur fossilised dung shows that herbivorous dinosaurs such as Euoplocephalus grazed conifers, tree ferns, mare's tail and ferns. Any parts of the plant not eaten but buried become fossilised by compression and their sap became amber. Partially fossilised resin is called copal.

Who is **galling** to **conifers?**

There are large populations of insects in coniferous forests but because conifer tissue tends to be hard, resinous, sticky and unpalatable, the insects cannot inflict damage. Just think, if you are an insect which likes to suck, the resin tends to block your fine mouthpart tube. For every preventative measure nature will produce a counterpart. When it comes to sap sucking the small spruce gall aphid, *Adelges abietis*, sips the juice of Norway spruce needles which in turn produces tell-tale needle malformation. Another aphid sounding like a shaver blade, *Gilletteela cooleyi*, sups on Sitka spruces, *Picea sitchensis*, and also migrates on to Douglas firs, *Pseudotsuga menziesii*. Pine twigs in the soft wood of new growth are prone to damaging sap-sucking by a tiny gall-mite, *Eriphyes pini*, leaving tell-tale lumpy swellings that also house its progeny long after the galls harden.

8

The Good, the Bad and the Ugly

What is **biodiversity?**

Frightened by the way humans use their planet, biologists invented this word to address and understand the world's myriad environments encompassing a healthy and mutually beneficial balance of micro-organisms, plants and animals. As relentless deforestation continues, especially in Amazonia, it is frightening to know that more than half of all species live in tropical forests. Plants provide vital links between micro-organisms and animals, native plant loss – algae and mosses to flowers and forests – can dangerously weaken the chain of beneficial balance.

What **plants** symbolise **good?**

Plants with orange, gold or yellow flowers or fruits. Oranges shaped like the sun with their sweetly scented white blossoms are especially representative of good and the powers of the sun. The word orange did not exist in European languages until its introduction from Asia with the name label *naranga*. Once established in a garden Mary's Gold, the *Calendula* marigold, flowers during almost every month of the year brightly symbolising the sun. Although much visited by bees, they do not see gold but, with their ultraviolet vision, blue. The artist's pigment, Indian yellow, was made in India from soil soaked in

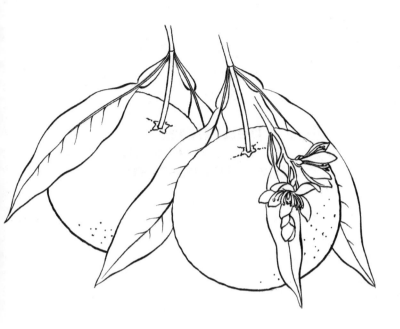

the urine of cows fed on mango leaves, it was finally banned as it made the sacred beasts ill.

Why **should** you remove **flowers** from a **bedroom** at **night?**

Because of reverse floral trading, or in simpler terms, during the hours of daylight flowers and plants remove carbon dioxide from the air and exhale oxygen but reverse the process at night. In addition, the scent of the Lily of the Valley, *Convallaria majalis*, is mildly noxious at night. A view over a garden is a safe and healthy option as researchers have found patients observing the flora and fauna outside get better quicker than those looking out onto buildings.

Why is it **beneficial** for most **plants** to have **fungus-root?**

The fungal threads that support ninety per cent of plants are called *mycorrhiza* – Greek for fungal roots, they secure a firm footing in the plants' roots working to ensure a mutually beneficial or symbiotic association with the soil. These threads or filaments radiate for miles from the roots, criss-crossing the soil trapping water and mineral nutrients to ensure plant vigour and health as well as survival under duress. Fortunately, *mycorrhiza* are adept foragers and travellers through the soil, enabling them to seek out the notoriously stay-at-home phosphate ions that are dietary essentials for flower and fruit formation.

Going back into the mists of time about 435 million years ago, fossil evidence at the dawning of the Silurian period suggests *mycorrhiza* assisted the evolutionary leap when plants first adapted themselves from pond life to that on inhospitable land. Initially, they were leafless and rootless spreading by rhizomes, a wandering underground or soil-surface storage organ, across the ground surface – great when it was damp, perilous as the ground dried out. So their evolution to putting down healthy roots was engineered and developed by the networking *mycorrhiza*.

What about **plants** without **fungus-root?**

Nettles can draw phosphates out of the richest soil without needing or forming mycorrhizal associations. The good news is that they are a clear indicator of where the good soil is in a garden.

Obviously plants such as mosses and liverworts, known as bryophytes, without roots but with stems and leaves, cannot use *mycorrhiza*. They turn to another Greek way of living – Poikilohydry which roughly translates as varied water. Mosses need to be pleasantly moist to photosynthesise so they literally adapt to varied water. When dry they turn their faces to the wall or the tree trunk, but in the spray zone of waterfalls, spring-fed shady banks and boggy marshes it is action stations. Carbon dioxide dissolves in the thin film of water over the mosses' leaves initiating the manufacture of light and air into sugar which feeds the mosses. When moist, mosses grow prolifically without heating or fermenting, and their spreading colonies and myriad microscopic leaves enable them to cling on to every last drop. Conversely, mosses can suffer 98 per cent desiccation and still survive: dried specimens in cabinets have been revived in water after forty years.

Where can I
find **Fairy** Rings?

Throughout the world where there is cultivated turf grass, especially if it is on lighter-textured soil and if thatch, a matted layer of dead stalks and moss, has been allowed to build up. There are big circles ranging from up to several hundred feet in diameter, to more delicate rings of just a few inches. If more than one develops, they tend to inhibit each other and end up just producing arcs in the grass. The circle is formed from any one of fifty different fungi, correctly called basidio-mycetes, some poisonous, some edible. Some fungi look like field mushrooms others like puffballs. They don't attack the grass as such, but tend to spring up around the stumps of felled or fallen trees and shrubs, where they change the chemistry and physical structure of the soil. One effect is that the soil becomes hydrophobic, literally hating water, in the sense that it becomes water repellent creating drought stress and possible death to the grass. On the other hand, one of the fungi, *Chlorophyllum*, is by name and nature green loving and releases nitrogen into the soil resulting in lush dark green grass.

How many **medicinal** plants are **there?**

Who knows? Scientists and researchers have examined less than 10 per cent of known plants for their possible medicinal value. Not only have we yet to fully identify the world's medicinal plants, there are still tribes of undiscovered people who have their own medicinal plant knowledge that could be of vital importance. Research is currently being undertaken by Glenn Shepard Jr with the Peruvian Metsigenka people who use about 270 indigenous plants for medicinal purposes. Have a look at the Latin names of plants in the house, garden and park – if they have the specific name *officinalis* it indicates they were once sold as medicinal plants and had commercial value in shops.

Which **plant** has a **root shaped** like a **man?**

Mandrake, *Mandragora officinalis* – good, bad and ugly, it enjoys a steamy reputation of death and dark deeds, and powerful medicine. Its old Arabic name of *Tuphac-el-Sheiton* translates as arousing voluptuous emotions and legend has it that it germinates from the last ejaculation of the hanged man. Rough

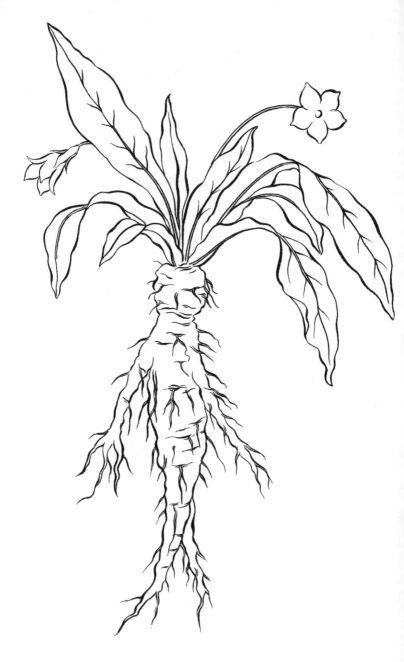

green leaves are followed by pale insignificant flowers that ripen into green golf ball fruits beneath which lie the human shaped roots. Legend warns that you lift the roots at your peril because as it leaves the earth, the plant emits a deadly shriek. Harvesters were advised to just loosen the soil and tie a rope around the leafy top, then find a dog and tie it to the other end of the rope: while carefully covering your ears you drove the dog away so that the root was torn from the ground. If by chance you heard the shriek your days were numbered as its sound was fatal. Shakespeare used the word mandrake when he was poisoning his cast but Mandragora when he was sending them into a deep sleep. More recent fictional use was made by J.K. Rowling in *Harry Potter and the Chamber of Secrets*: Professor Sprout equipped her class at Hogwarts with protective ear muffs before they set about the task of pricking out baby mandrakes, with the reassurance that, although dangerous, the cries of these juvenile seedlings would not be fatal.

Which **deadly plant** reveals the **patron** saint of **wizards?**

The *Actaea spicata*, baneberry or Herb Christopher which is a rare British native: alternative names are Troll's Berry in Norway, Witch's Plant, Devil's Berry in Germany and Devil's Grape in France. It is associated with Reprobus who was a giant troll, the rejected one, an ogre with the face of a dog who devoured men. It fell to Reprobus to control this 'killing plant' so beloved of witches, wizards, trolls and devils. However, virtue caught up with him and he was baptised, renamed Christopher and ordered to kill no more and he became the patron saint of wizards. His 'killing plant' was similarly converted and to this day the rootlets of the renamed Herb Christopher reveal in section a cross or a star.

What is the most poisonous plant?

Look for hemlock, Spotted Hemlock, *Conium maculatum*, which John Gerard described as '. . . one of the deadly poisons which killeth by his colde qualitie . . . ' – coldly lethal. The further south you travel, the more actively poisonous hemlock becomes, even breathing its scent can have narcotic effects. Children have died from using the stems as blow pipes or whistles. Before flowering the poisonous principle lies in the leaves, this diminishes when the plant is in fruit.

Why did Socrates choose to die from hemlock?

Your mind stays clear to the end but the process is horrifying. Salivation, bloating, dilation of the pupils and rolling of the eyes are followed by laboured respiration, diminished frequency of breathing and irregular heart action. This leads to loss of sensation, convulsions, uncertain gait, falling and finally complete paralysis.

Why do **birds** **eat** poisonous **yew** berries?

Birds happily devour the safe red flesh of yew berries, as fortunately their beaks are not hard enough to break the poisonous seeds. Eventually they pass through the bird's system dropping clean away from the parent plant in every sense. A Victorian schoolboy dare was to swallow the berry coating and spit out the seeds – not one to be tried out at home.

Which **plant** contains **cyanide?**

The young leaves of bracken contain cyanide which helps to ensure a safe start to its march across the countryside. The cyanide stops almost all insects' deleterious nibbling with the exception of the caterpillars of the saw fly and buff ermine moth. The cyanide in the young leaves is then replaced by a toxic cocktail in the older leaves which can cause blindness and cancer in rabbits and deer.

Which **plant** is more **deadly** than cobra **venom?**

The Castor Oil Plant, *Ricinus communis*, a magnificent bedding plant looking like an exotic triffid with its red furry palmate leaves and dramatic flowerheads, it is the seeds that contains the deadly poison ricin. The outer coating of the seeds is thick and leathery with a shining marble-grey and brown colouring within which is a thin, dark-coloured more brittle coat. Just three seeds are enough to kill an adult. It appears in the Bible as *kikayon*, the Hebrew for 'nauseous to the taste'; however, Jonah chose to rest in the safety of its shade between his trials with the whale.

Ricin was the poison that coated the tip of the umbrella that killed the Bulgarian Georgi Markov. It is also the source of the non-poisonous Castor Oil purgative popularly used by mothers trying to keep their children 'regular' in the early to mid-twentieth century.

What other **bedding** is good but **bad** and **dangerous** to know?

Sweetly scented, elegant and exotic the Angels Trumpets, *Datura*, come into their dangerously luminous own by evening or moonlight. If you put the flowers of Angel's Trumpets to your lips they are so poisonous it is said the next thing you will hear is angels trumpeting your arrival in paradise. The *Datura* commonly known as Thornapple is moth-pollinated. All parts, especially the fruit and flowers, are toxic, containing similar tropane alkaloids as Deadly Nightshade. Like henbane it has capsules rather than berries.

Its hallucinogenic properties were put to ancient sacred purposes by the Aztecs, the Native American Algonquin and possibly even the Delphic Sphinx. The subspecies *D. inoxia* subsp *inoxia* is the sacred *Datura* of the American Indians and was used in religious ceremonies for hallucinogenic effects. Closely related is the Jimsonweed, a corruption of Jamestown in Virginia where the early settlers inadvertently poisoned themselves on it. Its sweet scent belies its violently toxic constituents and skin irritant. It is sometimes grown as a source of alkaloidal drugs including atropine. On the other hand, gardeners are prepared to risk growing it in their borders for the brief pleasure of its trumpet shaped violet flowers that resemble Morning Glory.

Are all **Solanums** poisonous?

All Solanums contain the deleterious narcotic principle solanine so you need to watch which parts you eat. Plants in the solanum family include potatoes, tomatoes and aubergines as well as Deadly Nightshade, Henbane and Datura. In potatoes it is the green parts that are dangerous especially the leaves, however, it is also inadvisable to eat green potatoes. One wild species of South American potato protects itself from aphid depredation by discharging a pheromone that mimics that of aphids when under attack. Aubergines were described by the Tudor herbalist John Gerard as Madde or Raging Apples and eating them was 'such perill' and having 'a mischevious qualitie' that he advised against trying them. Turkish legend recounts that a priest fainted with gastronomical joy at the fragrant odour of cooked aubergines. As the twentieth century dawned William Robinson simply advised that they were best grown for ornamental value only.

Is **Monkshood,** Aconitum, a **dangerous** hoodie?

Yes, legend recounts that Hecate fashioned the first plants of *Aconitum* from the foaming saliva of the three headed Cereberus – legend does not mention from which mouth. Extracts were put on meat intended to lure and poison wolves hence one of its other names, Wolfsbane. *A. ferox* grows in the Himalayas and was used by Indians to poison spears, darts and arrows as well as destroying tigers. In times of invasion it was used to poison wells so as to slow down invading armies. The gentler name of Monkshood refers to the cowled shape of the flowers.

What **makes** a **Commiphora leaf** dangerous to **turn** over?

The leaf beetle, *Diamphidia nigroornata*, in Namibia use the leaves of *Commiphora* as a nursery host plant for their larvae. When the larvae feed on the leaves they produce a toxin which is collected by Kalahari Desert Bushmen and squeezed onto an arrow tip. Just one such poisoned arrow is enough to fell an adult antelope.

How do **plants** resist **attack** by **insects?**

Plants can produce a multitude of repellent chemicals, these substances are contained in their leaves and sap as well as forming an integral part of the scent and nectar. Substances include bitter, toxic alkaloids and tannins which repel by their scent or, if consumed by unwanted insects and other animals, will cause minor or major digestive malfunctions or even poisoning and death. Such resistance is at a high price to the plants, often weakening them, but evidence shows that there is an airborne jungle telegraph between plants under attack. At the warning whiff of danger, related plants close by engaging their resistance mechanisms.

The unattractive smell from a cabbage patch is a form of

mustard gas, closely related to mustard seed, its pungent flavour deters most animals from consuming it. Two components are held in specialist cells of the leaf: when the plant is attacked, mustard glucosinolate makes contact with an enzyme called myrosinase, and this releases a bitter isothiocyanate. Sadly, this acrid defence does not deter the Cabbage White Caterpillar which not only tolerates the bitter compound, but uses it to its own advantage. It incorporates the repellent isothiocyanate into its tissues so making it in turn distasteful to its predators. However, help is at hand for the cabbages; when under attack the danger scents they release mix and mingle with those of the caterpillar. This cocktail offers a sensory delight for the parasitic wasp *Cotesia glomerata* who flies in to feast.

Another serious pest of cabbage patches is the Mealy Cabbage greenfly which incorporates the mustard glucosinolate into its body but manufactures its own myrosinase. However, it is prey to a specialist greenfly parasitic wasp *Diaretiella rapae*: when this predator crushes the greenfly, it releases the isothiocyanate and the alarm pheromone farnesene that signal other greenfly to leave the area. Pity non-native crop and garden plants that have been introduced around the globe without their native guardians so their cries for help go unheeded.

Can **Sweet Gale**
blow insects **away?**

Yes and no: its distinctive scent and flavour are used to both repel insects and flavour beer in the Scottish Highlands where it grows freely. It is a small shrub, growing to about 90cm in boggy acid soils, hence its other name Bog Myrtle. There are male and female plants, the former have spike flowers that look like catkins and the latter short ellipse shaped spikes. The male discharges the anemophilous pollen from his anthers to blow away on the wind until it falls on the nearby female spikes. Remarkably the trees that bear flowers of one sex during one year, may bear the other for the next year. After flowering, the narrow serrated leaves appear dotted with the aromatic oil-bearing glands.

Recent research has discovered that the oil extracted from the leaves of Sweet Gale, *Myrica gale*, is four times more effective at killing acne bacteria than any product currently on the market. For years its cultivation and harvest have been undertaken on a modest scale in Scotland, in Argyll and the Spey valley. However, in order to fulfil the potentially huge demand to banish acne, vast acreages are being cleared. It is estimated that by 2013, 5,000 hectares will be under cultivation in fields extending into the Scottish Borders, Moray and Aberdeenshire.

On a smaller scale, the Royal Botanic Gardens in Edinburgh have used the native Sweet Gale in the centre of a memorial garden for Queen Elizabeth the Queen Mother, in remembrance of her ancestry and lifelong links with Scotland. Its winter garden has had new life breathed into it around a central labyrinth based on the Celtic cross.

Why do **some** fruits smell **sour,** musty, cabbage-like or **sickly?**

To attract fruit-eating bats to visit, dine on and digest their fruit, later spreading their seeds. Bats are drawn by sight and smell so the fruit wafts a bat reproductive perfume. In 1792 Thomas Bewick in *The History of Quadrapeds* described the Rousette or Great Ternate Bat as feeding on fruits with a partiality for palm fruits on which they gorged until intoxicated, sometimes falling to the ground.

Can a **banana** unzip **itself?**

Yes: a banana that originated in north-east India, the *Musa velutina*, when ripe literally opens along its skin seams to reveal a creamy white luscious sweet banana. Unfortunately this banana contains very hard black seeds – so it is no good for commercial production. The commercially edible bananas are from the Cavendish cultivars of *M. x paradisiaca* which have been developed so as not to have seeds. *Musa* is named for Antonius Musa, physician to the first Roman Emperor, Octavius Augustus, its Arab name is *mauz*.

What makes cleavers stick to my clothes?

Cleavers, also known as goosegrass and sticky-willy, is the common name for *Galium aparine*. It has small hook-like hairs on its stems and leaves which enable it to tenaciously scramble through grass and hedges – not to mention passing humans! After flowering it produces similarly bristly fruits which are by far the worst, they cling to clothes and the fur of passing animals, an inconvenience which helps them spread their seed. The hook-like hairs were the inspiration for Velcro.

Where can a mouldy wedge of sedge aid concentration?

In the Manu National Park in Peru, this sedge known locally as *ivenkiki* suffers from a fungal attack which ruins its fruits and flowers as well as leaving the bulb infected with an alkaloid. Local people chew the bulb as a stimulant and enhancer of concentration. A rather different effect from *ivenkiki* sedge chewing is experienced by Norway lemmings in the Arctic

Tundra. The indigenous sedges and cotton grass are an important part of the lemming's grazing food because they contain a poison which neutralises their digestive juices. If lemming populations are low, the grazing is comparatively light and the effects wear off after 30 hours.

When the lemming numbers are higher, feeding is more frenzied and the effects multiply, leaving the lemmings continually in a state of near starvation. In a bid to find better feeding they take to the waters to seek new land – drowning en masse.

Can you **take** the **fever** out of **hay?**

Grass pollen is notorious for setting off sneezing fits in hay fever sufferers but help is at hand, Australian researchers have developed a 'sneeze-free' grass. Using a 'gene silencing' technology they have 'silenced' two culprit allergenic proteins in a new strain of rye grass. The same technology is being used on other grasses such as ornamental tall fescues, leaving us free to roam the prairie clear eyed and dry nosed. Good news for browsers as well as it is more nutritious and easily digestible, the latter should help in the battle to lower methane emissions from grazing herds.

Why are **only** the lower **leaves** of holly **prickly?**

The more tender younger leaves of holly would be grazed by wild animals if they did not have painful prickles. However, the young shoots of holly are said to be a tonic for rabbits.

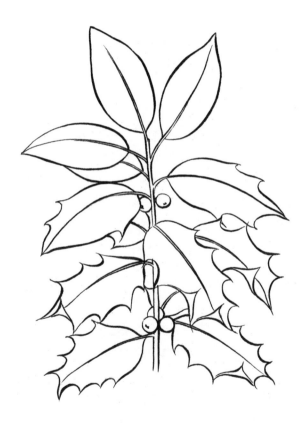

Why is the **holly** the **cleanest** tree in the **wood?**

The medieval answer was that no man doth wipe his arse upon it.

How can a **neatly** clipped **yew** **hedge** help cancer **sufferers?**

Gardens and landscapes with long yew hedges are now saving their clippings and sending them to be processed to extract Taxol. Taxol, which is used to fight breast and ovarian cancer, was first discovered in the bark of the Pacific yew tree, *Taxus brevifolia*, which grows in the Pacific north-west of North America. Limited supplies slowed the development of its extraction until it was also identified in the common yew, *Taxus baccata*.

Which **seeds** have saved **sperm** whales?

A tree in the Euphorbia family, the Jojoba, *Simmondsia chinensis*. The oil was first pressed from the seeds as a substitute for the oil of sperm whales known as spermaceti. The oil is resistant to oxidation so can be used as a lubricant, a polish or, if mixed with other oils and wax, to make a water-resistant coating. The demand has now extended to shampoos, lotions and sunblocks.

What does a **shark's liver** have in **common** with a tree **bark?**

A molecule called squalamine which was first isolated in the liver of the dogfish shark. Squalamine is a naturally occurring steroid which fights cancer by cutting off the blood flow to tumours. The deciduous trees *Holarrhena* which grow in Asia and Africa as well as the sweet scented climber *Conemorpha macrophylla*, which grows from Java to the foothills of the Himalayas, both contain substances very similar to squalamine. This substance evolved as a defence mechanism against predators. Extracts have been used by traditional Ayurvedic practitioners in India: *Holarrhena* to combat dysentery and *C. macrophylla* to treat skin disorders.

Can the **African** spider **flower** help control **spider** mites?

Scientists hope so. The African spider flower, *Cleome gynandra*, has long been known to repel pests. Work has been undertaken experimenting with extracts from *C. gynandra* and it is believed that a working extract has now been created which we will be able to use to control spider mites.

Is **there** any **merit** in a **dandelion** clock?

Only very roughly. On a hot day the downy seeds lose moisture and their grip on the seedhead, therefore, at two, three, four and five in the afternoon on a hot day they may well be accurate.

9

On this Planet and beyond

If the **Earth** is **more** than 4,500 **million** years old, **what** is the **earliest** evidence of **plant** life?

As the molten earth cooled the water vapour condensed and formed rivers and seas capable of hosting primitive life in a barren landscape with a noxious atmosphere. Fossilised bacteria 3,200 million years old have been dated from rocks in southern Africa and as plant cells evolved into seaweeds or green algae they added oxygen to the atmosphere. And so it continued, give or take a million years, from the Precambrian, when the Ancient Life Era starts, through Cambrian and Ordovician geological divisions, until the dawning of the Silurian period about 435 million years ago when plants first adapted themselves to life on land, albeit leafless. After 40 million years of this which included the arrival of the first insects 410 million years ago, there followed 50 million years of the Devonian period, then the Carboniferous or coal age dawned. It forms part of the Palaeozoic or Primary Era when plant life was mostly made up of ferns and mosses growing in its largely warm and moist climate. Ferns can be classed as the first to appreciate private pools: they used them to reproduce. Their fronds produced wind-dispersed spores which as they landed and spread into small pools, produced eggs at one end and sperm the other

– in much the same way as mosses do today, (see p. 24). The sperm swam across to do their duty fertilising the eggs and up sprang new ferns. Coastlands were coated in thick layers of swamp vegetation created by the pattern of flooding and then receding waters so that they were alternately buried under marine deposits and then reformed. As the Carboniferous era continued the climate fostered giant evergreen trees, huge tree ferns, massive club mosses and towering horsetails which in time fell and rotted. These layers of alternating decayed compressed vegetation hardened to form coal and sedimentary rocks such as Carboniferous limestone and sandstone. In North America the Carboniferous rocks are known by their geographical distribution – Mississippian and Pennsylvanian. Gymnosperms vaulted into action around 290 million years ago producing seeds that were no longer reliant on water and opening the era of cycads, ginkgos – the maidenhair ferns, conifers and seed ferns.

About 130 million years ago flowering plants, the angiosperms, first adorned the earth as dinosaurs became extinct. More innovative than the earlier gymnosperms they produced varying seed that would evolve and adapt to climate and environmental changes. They also produced grasses about 15 million years ago that developed nourishing ears to feed the planet.

How did the **Ice Age** affect plants in **Europe** and North **America?**

As the impenetrable ice sheets and glaciers engulfed the northern continents the indigenous flora was driven southwards. Finally as the Ice Age warmed and the glaciers retreated many plants started to recolonise. In Europe the Alps acted as an east-west barrier, stopping what are now called 'Mediterranean' plants from returning to their native habitats further north. However, the mountain ranges in North America run north-south creating an ice free corridor between present day Alaska and the Mississippi basin, pockets of tender plants were carried far further north on receding glaciers. An example of this is the Monterey pine, *Pinus radiata*, originating only on the Monterey peninsula of western North America, its seeds having been left by the retreating glaciers (see pp. 86-7).

Where is the **'deadest'** soil in the **world?**

The Yungay region of the Atacama Desert in Chile which has only 2 per cent of the moisture of either the Sahara Desert or California's Death Valley. Soil scientists have observed that its characteristics and reactions closely resemble the Martian soil gathered by astronauts in 1976, as there are limitless quantities of Yungay Region soil. In principle if anything can be made to grow or any trace of life is found in this earthly soil, the results could be applied to establishing life on Mars.

Can **plants** live inside **rocks?**

In Antarctica scientists have identified the layers of green and white about a sixteenth of an inch under the rock surface as a living trio of algae, fungi, and bacteria colonising the damp spaces between crystals of porous sandstone. The algal species is *Hemichloris antarctica* seemingly insensitive to freezing and thawing. Scientists believe this may replicate the last footholds of life on drying and cooling Mars.

How could **plants** **grow** on other **planets?**

Life on other planets is being examined by the Maryland Astrobiology Consortium using species of micro-organisms, microbes called *Archaea* taken from an Antarctic lake in the same circumstances as the previous answer. They huddle together to form a chemically linked biofilm, a microbial mat (see p. 11) which might be mirrored in the liquid frozen under the surface of Mars. Aggregating to form a mat allows the microbes to share nutrients and genetic material. This is plant life at its most primitive but a link has been established and waits to be proved with findings on Mars and potentially some of the 180 recently discovered small planets revolving around other stars in the universe or on their terrestrial moons.

At the opposite end of the spectrum, David Darling has written about the discovery of extremophiles, bacteria that live in sulphurous hot springs, deep inside the earth, and at the bottom of oceans. They do not derive their energy from the sun but use the heat coming from within the earth to metabolise. Darling has interpreted his researches to argue that life in general, of which plant life is a part, does not have to exist or begin in conditions such as there are, or indeed have been, on the surface of the earth, but can thrive in places previously believed to be hostile to life. So it is a case of yes there is plant life but not as we know it.

Can I **grow** ancient **seeds?**

Yes in principle, but most ancient seeds need first to be raised in controlled conditions and then their progeny can be distributed. The John Innes Institute in Norwich donated 'Mummy Peas' to The Heritage Seed Library at Ryton: they were believed to have been found in a sealed jar in an Egyptian pyramid in a Pharaoh's tomb by an archaeologist, Mr. Grimstone, during the 1840s. This proved to be a profitable history as he sold them at ten for 5s (25p) complete with an information leaflet. The Pharoah's Peas available today as heritage seeds were supposedly found in the tomb of Tutankhamun. Their most recent verified history pinpoints a 1920s variety taken from Lord Caernarvon's garden at Highclere in Berkshire which he may well have brought back from Tutankhamun's tomb. However, 3,000 year old pea seeds have been grown by Suzuka Municipal Museum of Archaeology in Japan; they have purple flowers and their green peas turned rice pink.

What is the 'doomsday vault'?

It is a subterranean global seed bank at Svalbard, Norway, inside the Arctic Circle's permafrost zone. It is large enough to hold a global seed bank of some 3 million varieties of vital crops. Wakehurst Place, a satellite of the Royal Botanic Gardens, Kew, houses the Millennium Seed Bank which also operates at sub-zero temperatures enabling seeds to retain their viability for decades. The Millennium Seed Bank aims to collect and conserve seed from all the United Kingdom's native flowering plant species and 10 per cent of the world's species with a special emphasis on dry tropical regions.

What is a **moon cereus?**

It is a nocturnal cactus, *Selenicereus*, whose fragrant elusive flowers appear for one night but not every year. In their native surroundings they either climb trees and hang with aerial roots or, in rocky terrains and cliffs, simply scramble across. The botanical artist Margaret Mee hunted down the flowers for years before being able to paint them in 1988, the last and eightieth year of her life. The legendary journey up the River Negro was undertaken in a boat with a fifty year old diesel engine. By dusk they reached the Parana Anavilhanas – an emerald green landscape splashed with brilliant colours dominated by huge tropical trees rising from the waters, draped in bromeliads and philodendrons and wild orchids. The next morning, the voyage proved not to be in vain with the discovery of a large tree enclosed by thorny bushes on which grew *S. wittii* with three buds. The moonlit vigil started the next night, as daylight dimmed into the light of the full moon, one petal on one bud started to open, followed by another and another. The open flower filled the air with an extraordinary sweet perfume and Mee painted four blossoms, each 10in long and 5in wide, the fifth beginning to fade. They had twelve pure white petals and over fifty white sepals and gold tipped anthers and, like the undersides of leaves of so many tropical plants, the sepals were backed with a maroon tint.

The eminently readable American garden writer, Peter Loewer, describes his encounter with *S. grandiflorus* with contagious excitement: 'In the West Indies this flower is called the king of the night and of all the nocturnal flowers I've seen, this is one of the most dramatic, especially since it possesses a powerful fragrance touched with vanilla. The floral cup is over ten inches wide with petals and sepals of pure white inside and tinges of salmon without. The stems are an inch thick and a light gray-green to purple in color'. No surprise that the other common names are Goddess of the Night and Princess of the Night.

Why don't seeds germinate in moonlight?

They do not germinate because the red part of the light spectrum is missing. So if the weeds in your garden have all gone to seed help is at hand: the maxim 'one year's weed, seven years seed' can be controlled – dig on moonlit evenings. A weed seed has only to be exposed to a moment's daylight as the soil turns to germinate as opposed to resting dormant if exposed to moonlight.

Should I sow seeds by the phases of the moon?

As the moon has the strength to control the ebb and flow of the ocean's tides, why not the way the water in the ground affects plant's growth? General advice includes sowing peas and beans as the moon wanes to give them a rest before germinating. The waxing moon provides a more glowing light that enhances the golden hues in spring plants. The full moon fattens up cucumbers, horseradish, leeks, lilies, radishes, saffron and turnips. The magnificent 'Harvest Moon' that occurs nearest to the autumnal equinox gained its name because its light enabled the harvest to continue after sunset.

Why are **white** and **grey** plants more **visible** by **moonlight?**

The light of the full moon is only 1/600,000th part of the sun's light. The moon only reflects about one tenth of the sunlight that falls upon it, the rest being absorbed by the lunar surface. In turn, the earth reflects to the moon about fourteen times as much light as the moon sends to earth because of the light reflected from the oceans and clouds of the world. Our

eyes have rods in the periphery that only see black and white while the eyes' central cones detect colours such as reds and purples. A nineteenth-century scientist Johannes Evangelista Purkinje discovered this and demonstrated that in dim light, i.e. at dusk, the ability to see red and green disappears and we are left with blue and yellow plus black, white, and shades of grey. As evening draws on the yellows fade but we can still see the brightness of white which remains, giving the illusion of a black sky of twinkling white lights and clear moon above and luminescent pale flowers and leaves below. The blazing floral reds of daytime are reduced to black holes. Apart from having night scent this is why so many bat and nocturnally pollinated flowers are white or pale.

The mauve flowers of Honesty are reasonably luminescent but it gets its Latin name, *Lunaria*, from its lunar shaped seed discs that shine in moonlight.

Why is the **flora** on **islands** often **unique?**

Originally the world was formed into two ancient continents; Laurasia and most importantly, the southerly Gondwanaland. According to the continental drift theory Gondwanaland split into most of Africa, Madagascar, India, Australia, Antarctica and parts of South America, with a range of habitats where flowering plants developed as the atmosphere changed. When the continents split, islands were also formed separated by seas and oceans from mainland human and animal depredations. These islands preserved species in isolation that had grown on the original landmasses – a continental parallel is the Tepuy mountains, Conan Doyle's *Lost World*, in Venezuela. In New Guinea the forest wilderness has survived because it has never been colonised by monkeys or other large mammals and it provides a sheltered habitat for a panoply of reptiles, marsupials and birds.

Did **comets** bring **nitrogen** to earth?

On 15 January 2006 an artificial meteorite lit up the night sky. It was the returning Stardust probe which brought to Earth a thousand grains of dust from the comet Wild 2. The dust included a rich stock of organic compounds, including two that contained biologically usable nitrogen. Scientists are asking if this is further proof that comets played a role in the emergence of Earth. They had previously assumed planets amassed 'local' materials but how could particles stray so far from the sun. Nitrogen occupies by volume some 78 per cent of dry air and is the most abundant gas in the atmosphere; although it is chemically inactive it serves to dilute oxygen. The atmosphere that surrounds earth is an envelope of air consisting principally of a mixture of gases: as well as Nitrogen, there is Oxygen forming 21 per cent, and a final 1 per cent includes Argos, Helium and a variable quantity of water vapour. Nitrogen fixing legume crops such as peas help, as they convert nitrogen from the air into the soil and into organic matter through nodules on their roots which enters the soil when they die. Healthy plant growth relies on Nitrogen (N) as one of the macronutrients in the soil with Phosphorus (P), Potassium (K), Magnesium (Mg), Calcium (Ca) and Sulphur (S). Nitrogen is the nutrient needed in the greatest quantity by most plants; it is essential for healthy green leaf vegetables and can help root development. This organic matter is stored in the earth but it has to be mineralised to inorganic ions by the activity of soil bacteria before it is available to plants – growing legumes short cuts this lengthy process.

So just **what** other **secrets** do the **Stardust** grains **contain?**

To date none of the meteorites that have fallen to earth have contained chemicals unknown to man.

Will **man** garden on **Venus?**

Venus has been described as Earth's sister, her unruly twin. Like Earth's landforms, it was formed by volcanic and deformation processes but rent by rift valleys, scarred by comets and asteroids, and blackened by seas of hardened lava. The oozing lava has created 'pancakes' very similar to those found in California except that Venus's remain pristine and California's have fillings of plants growing where wind and water erosion has occurred. The prospect on Venus is hardly propitious in terms of growing plants. If conditions change much can be achieved, for one Venutian day is the equivalent to 243 of our earthly days. In the meantime every gardener wanting to create a night garden can count on Venus enhancing their plots. When she shines in the evenings then she is very bright indeed and clearly visible in the western sky.

If **coal** was once a **tree** why does **burning** it now **pollute** the **atmosphere?**

Coals consist largely of non-crystalline carbon, although of organic origin i.e. from decayed trees and other vegetable matter. They were growing when the world's atmosphere was unsustainable for human life. Coal fires release the pollutant gases and hydrocarbon chemicals that have been stored since the Carboniferous Age. Burning wood, on the other hand, does not pollute because the gases and chemicals that have formed its growth are the same as ours and the resultant smoke can be absorbed without pollution. Effectively it just releases compatible gases back into the environment. Wood ash is a valuable source of potash; young wood yields about 15 per cent potash whereas older, thicker wood varies between 4 and 5 per cent. You can sprinkle it directly around flowering and fruiting plants as potash provides 'artificial sunshine', however, the nutrients are more stable if recycled in layers on a compost heap. Bonfires are greeted with a mixed reception; the ash is good if composted but composting most of the material rather than burning it would be of greater horticultural and environmental use, not forgetting neighbourhood popularity. Tree seeds often germinate better if leaves from their parent plant are included in the seed compost because the leaves help set up a mutually beneficial fungal link with the soil known as mycorrhizal association (see pp. 220-1).

Can it **rain** plants?

Just as you are unlikely to see cats and dogs falling from the skies, 'Millet Rains' in East Africa are actually one of the two maximum rainfalls experienced between October and December, so called because they are vital to good yields of the staple crop millet. One of the two heaviest rainfalls between February and May is known as the Maize Rains which unsurprisingly helps the maize to be as high as an elephant's eye.

Could **plants** eat **humans?**

Some plant names suggest that they could but in reality not at the moment. The *Paphiopedilum callosum* has the common name of Triffid Orchid and there are also Dracula orchids in existence.

Would they be **able** to digest us?

Carnivorous plants can dissolve insects, small frogs and other beasties but genetic modification of these plants would have to be on a gargantuan scale for them to eat or dissolve humans.

How did **plants** lure **tyrannosaurs** to **help** them?

In the Cretaceous period flowering plants began to develop fruits rich in sugars to encourage tyrannosaurs to eat the fruit and thus disperse their seeds. Some fruits might have started fermenting providing the added bonus of a little light inebriation.

Which **plants** have a **touch** of **glass?**

These are the true gems of the ocean, the diatoms, of which there are over 70,000 species. They are single-celled algae found in fresh water and oceans with fantastic glass shells which they build in complex patterns. You would need a microscope or even better a scanning electron microscope to view them properly. Small but perfectly formed, about 25,000,000 would fit in a teaspoon. Diatoms have brought manifold benefits to the planet. They make up at least a quarter of plant life by weight and produce at least a quarter of the oxygen we breathe; they

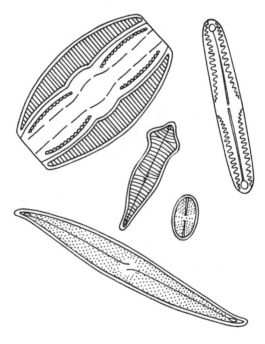

provide essential nutrition for animals ranging from protozoans to whales. Some species reproduce by simple cell division, others sexually. When diatoms die, their microscopic bodies fall to the ocean floor, where their oil-rich plasma eventually forms petroleum deposits. Their skeletons are mined for use as filters and abrasives. Biologists use diatoms to identify sources of water pollution and oversee the health of ecosystems whilst geologists use them to reconstruct historical climate patterns. Biologist (and enthusiast) Edward Theriot adds further extraordinary uses for diatoms tracers in military intelligence, evidence connecting criminals to crime scenes, and pointers to the location of drownings and in archaeology to indicate the sources of clay used in pottery.

What plant **cuts** like **glass?**

The construction size bamboo, *Dendrocalamus giganteus*, which has hairs in its leaf sheaths that cut like glass. It was used traditionally in oriental tortures.

Where was **terrestrial paradise?**

The garden 'east of Eden' commonly known as The Garden of Eden. Alexander the Great, Sir John Mandeville and many others believed that it was the source of both the Nile and the Ganges and that it was among mountains higher than the moon on the far side of India. Medieval maps of the world always included the Garden of Eden at the top as east was used on early maps where modern maps use polar north. This practice is the origin of the word orientation; you used the map to establish east or the orient. Paradise comes from the Persian word paradeisos meaning an enclosed park, used for hunting but adorned with trees, roses and other sweet smelling flowers. A man made contrast to the barren rigours of the surrounding untamed landscape.

Bibliography

Attenborough, David *The Private Life of Plants* (BBC Books, 1995)

Blunt, Wilfred *In for a Penny: A Prospect of Kew Gardens* (Hamish Hamilton, 1978)

Bodkin, Frances *Encyclopedia Botanica The Essential Reference Guide to Nature and Exotic Plants in Australia* (Angus & Robertson, 1986)

Bown, Deni *The Royal Horticultural Society Encyclopedia of Herbs* (Dorling Kindersley, 1995)

Capon, Brian *Botany for gardeners An introduction and Guide* (Batsford, 1994)

Cothran, James R. *Gardens and Historic Plants of the Antebellum South* (University of South Carolina Press, 2003)

DeMouthe, Jean Frances *Natural Materials: Sources, Properties and Uses* (Architectural Press, 2006)

Erickson, Rica *Plants of Prey* (University of Western Australia Press, 1978)

Fairley, Alan *Seldom Seen Rare Plants of Greater Sydney* (Reed New Holland, 2004)

Friend, Rev. *Hilderic Flowers and Flower Lore* (Sonnenschein, 1886)

Holm, Eigil *The Biology of Flowers* (Penguin, 1979)

Hughes, Ted *Tales from Ovid* (Faber and Faber, 1997)

Hutchison, John *Common Wild Flowers* (Pelican, 1948)

Hutchison, John *Uncommon Wild Flowers* (Pelican, 1950)

Jong, Erica *Witches* (Granada, 1982)

Kimmerer, Robin Wall *Gathering Moss: A Natural and Cultural History of Mosses* (Oregon State University Press, 2003)

Knight, A.E. and Step, E.F.L.S. *Hutchinson's Popular Botany Vols I and II* (Hutchinson & Co.)

Lehner, Ernst and Johanna *Folklore and Odysseys of Food and Medicinal Plants* (Farrar, Straus, Giroux, 1973)

Lewis III, A. Jefferson *Historic, Heritage and Heirloom Plants of Georgian and the American South* (The University of Georgia, 2004)

Leyel, C.F. *Green Medicine* (Faber and Faber, 1952)

Loewer, Peter *The Evening Garden: Flowers and Fragrance from Dusk till Dawn* (Macmillan, 1993)

O'Hare, Mick (ed.) *Does Anything Eat Wasps? And 101 Other Questions* (New Scientist, 2005)

Otte, Jean Pierre *Love in the Garden* (Braziller, 2000)

Parker, Geoffrey (ed) *Atlas of World History* 4th ed. (BCA with Times Books, 1994)

Shephard, Sue *Seeds of Fortune: A Gardening Dynasty* (Bloomsbury, 2003)

Stearn, William T. *A Gardener's Dictionary of Plant Names* (Cassell, 1972)

Stickland, Sue *Heritage Vegetables The Gardener's Guide to Cultivating Diversity* (Gaia, 1998)

Talalaj, Prof. S, Talalaj D & J *The Strangest Plants in the World*
(Hale, 1991)

Toussaint-Samat, Maguelonne *History of Food*   (Bordas,
1987)

Out of Eden: The Eden Project Companion (Eden Project
Books, 2005)

The New Royal Horticultural Society Dictionary of Gardening
Vols. 1-4 (London, 1992)

Waring, Philippa *A Dictionary of Omens and Superstitions*
(Souvenir Press, 1978)

Vavilov, N.I. *Five Continents* (International Plant Genetic
Resources Institute, 1997)

Magazines and papers

Microbiology Today

National Geographic

New Phytologist

New Scientist

Seed News Heritage Seed Library

The Garden

The Organic Way

Vann, Stephen Dr. 'Fairy Ring of Turfgrass' paper published by
Agriculture and Natural Resources, University of Arkansas
Division of Agriculture